FROM STAGE FRIGHT TO THE ART OF GOOD LISTENING . . .

here are the total dynamics of the art of communicating: problems, pitfalls, prizes. No matter what your fears and self-doubts, you can become an effective public speaker and discover increased self-confidence, enthusiasm, poise, and self-knowledge.

Someday you, too, will be asked to speak before a school, church, community or political group. Here is a survival kit for both the *public* and *private* you!

". . . One of the most interesting, readable, well-written books on public speaking that has come out in a long time."

—*Baptist Record*

HOW TO SPEAK
SO PEOPLE WILL LISTEN

HOW TO SPEAK
SO PEOPLE WILL LISTEN

by Ronald L. Willingham

A Key-Word Book
Word Books, Publishers
Waco, Texas

HOW TO SPEAK SO PEOPLE WILL LISTEN

A KEY-WORD BOOK
Published by Pillar Books for Word Books, Publishers

First Key-Word edition published December 1976

ISBN: 0-87680-824-0

Library of Congress Catalog Card Number: 68-31119

Printed in the United States of America

graphic design by ANTHONY BASILE

Acknowledgement is gratefully given to the following publishers for brief excerpts from copyrighted works:

Harper and Row, Publishers
  From *The Art of Readable Writing* by Rudolf F. Flesch. Copyright 1949.

Standard Publishing Company
  From *The New Dictionary of Thoughts* by Tryon Edwards. Copyright 1964.

Division of Christian Education,
National Council of the Churches of Christ
  Quotations from *The Revised Standard Version of the Bible*. 1946, 1952.

DEDICATION

To all the men who have been in my development classes—this book is dedicated.

It's because of you that I have written it—you have given me inspiration, encouragement, and example.

And so, this isn't solely my book—much of it belongs to you.

Thank you and God bless you!

CONTENTS

ACKNOWLEDGEMENTS

It's appropriate that I take a separate page to say "thanks" to five people—five people who, in a very special way, have helped with this little book.

First, to Mrs. Ruth Haynes for reading, correcting, and typing the manuscripts. I appreciate so much the interest and friendship that she showed by the giving of her time.

Second, to Joe Barnett for his encouragement and early comments; but mainly for his friendship, counsel, and inspiration. These have helped change my life.

And then there's Beverly, Robin, and Becky who have understood that it takes many hours at the office to put a book together.

Thanks to all of you!

PREFACE

One evening, Don Chaney, a young radio advertising salesman stood in one of my classes and challenged the men with this question: "Who says that a picture is worth a thousand words?"

Then, before anyone could answer, he continued: "You give me a thousand words and I'll take the Lord's Prayer, the Twenty-Third Psalm, the Hippocratic Oath, a sonnet by Shakespeare, the Preamble to the Constitution, Lincoln's Gettysburg address, and I'll still have enough words left over for just about all of the Boy Scout Oath. Now would you trade these one thousand words for any picture?"

Well, Don had proved his point. At least, he convinced me of the importance of spoken words—and he convinced me with words. Now I'm telling you this to convince you of the importance of your words.

It's been said before in many ways, and by many wise men; but let me emphasize the truth again—success usually follows our ability to express ourselves efficiently. Or, as Dwight Watkins once wrote, "The ability to speak clearly and forcefully, whether in business or in social life, will do more to help you gain success than anything else in the world."

Sounds important, doesn't it? And of course it is!

The chances are that you are a person who speaks to groups of people. You may conduct a sales meeting, teach a Sunday school class, or preside at a civic club luncheon. You may tell a story to four or five people during a coffee break. But whatever the occasion, it's important that you learn to express yourself effectively.

And that's what this book is all about, that's why it was written—to help you express yourself more effectively!

Chapter One

If you want to learn to speak, you must realize the importance

"And God said, 'Let there be light,' and there was light."

God spoke creation into existence. That day speech created light; today speech creates *enlightenment*.

As our society grows and becomes more complex, so grows the need for effective speech. Goods are to be produced and services rendered, and this implies the motivation of people. The world's maladies need The Physician. This demands speech, for "how can they learn without a preacher?" Parents and children must communicate for the existence of healthy homes. So then, the ability to express oneself should be at the top of the list of every person. It's vital in every facet of our lives.

Sir Walter Raleigh recognized the importance of effective speech when he penned these words, "In all that ever I observed, I ever found that men's fortunes are oftener made by their tongues than by their virtues, and more men's fortunes overthrown thereby, also, than by their vices." The great English poet, Percy Bysshe Shelley, once commented, "He gave man speech, and speech created thought, which is the measure of the universe." It's obvious that these outstanding men considered speech vital.

How vital is speech in your life? Are you a salesman, an accountant, or a farmer? Does your livelihood depend on other people? Would your standard of living increase if you improved your ability to put your thoughts into words? Would your Christian service improve? Would you feel better and act with more confidence? There are exceptions, but usually success in any area of life follows your ability to express yourself effectively.

Look around you. See who are the successful individuals. Isn't the success of the teacher measured by his ability to transfer thoughts into his pupils' minds? The salesman's enthusiasm rubs off onto his prospects, and this governs his income. The minister's words of truth and sincerity mold and shape your life. *The dynamic leader is the person who expresses himself most effectively.* All your life you have desired these traits. Haven't you?

Because of speech, the early day Christians received the calming words of Christ. And this was necessary for us to have the written Word today. If there had been no emotion-filled speeches by such men as Patrick Henry, this nation might still be a colony. Hitler used public speaking to work his people into a frenzy of hate and hostility. The spoken word has had a mighty impact upon us, and the destiny of many people lies with its use. But the important question is how will *you* use it? How effective will *your* use be?

Being human, you have visualized yourself standing before a group of people, swaying them with your words. You have watched your minister preach and mentally placed yourself in his shoes. Unfortunately, while you would like to be in the speaker's shoes, you probably think it's impossible, don't you? You've always thought that speakers were born and not made. Haven't you? Well, I have good news for you. You can train yourself to become an effective speaker—a person who naturally puts his thoughts into words. You can, if you want to! But you must have a burning desire.

If you want to learn to speak, you must have a burning desire!

The overwhelming desire to speak publicly was the secret of Abraham Lincoln's achievements. His appetite for this trait started him down the road of historical prominence as nothing else would have done. He had no formal education, but he spoke at every opportunity. When he had no opportunity, he spoke to trees and fence posts. For many years he was a ne'er-do-well, but somehow he found time for public expression. After the death of Ann Rutledge he often contemplated suicide, yet even in times like this he kept the desire of public speaking before him. He practiced and studied. He dreamed. And this man, with ghastly physical features and whose clothes hung sloppily, was to utter the greatest classic in American history. Why? Because he had a burning desire.

Lincoln had many drawbacks that you'll never have. In overcoming these, he found strength. Only through exercise can you gain strength. Your strength will be in direct proportion to your desire. If it were possible for me to inject a serum into your veins that would insure your success as a speaker, it would be the serum of *desire*. Desire is greater than native ability or brilliance. So, to answer your question, "Can I really learn to speak in public?", the answer is a resounding *yes!* Yes, you can, if you really want to.

Today hundreds of men have enrolled in speech training classes. They have a strong desire to develop their abilities. Most of them say they want to express themselves in a clear and logical manner. They want to be better salesmen, accountants, or teachers. They simply want to stand on their two feet and say what's on their minds. Often they don't really believe that they are capable of doing this. To them it's just a dream.

As the weeks pass and time exposes their desires, miracles begin to happen. Possibly one or two fellows, not wanting to expose their true desires, will drop out of the class. But the majority grit their teeth and smash stage fright head-on. These are the men to whom I can say, "Yes, you will learn to organize your thoughts and speak on your feet." They are assured of success, whether they are bank tellers, farmers, truck drivers, or crane operators. There are no "born speakers." You train yourself to become one.

And training calls for desire and persistence. If you were a robot, you would probably have a series of gauges in your chest. If the cover of your desire gauge was opened and a reading taken, an exact measurement of your success as a speaker would be indicated. This would show the exact degree of your accomplishment. The point is, if I could measure your desire, I could determine almost exactly your success as a speaker. But then, you are reading this book because you already have a burning desire. So, let's get on to the next speaking skill.

If you want to learn to speak, you must be conversational

Today's successful speakers are successful because they're natural and conversational. In short, they're just themselves. They don't assume a stiff and artificial stage appearance. Can you think of anything more natural for a cowboy to do than to stand slumped, hat pushed back, spinning a rope? He has a grin on his face, which radiates informality, and casually discusses the events of the day.

Informality was the secret of the late Will Rogers, and millions loved him for being himself. He knew how to communicate with people. He knew how to sell his product. But then, if you're an Eastern advertising executive and try to spin a rope and talk with a Western twang, you won't succeed. It wouldn't be natural for you. Most beginners think that public speaking is a rigid form of stiffly copied gestures.

Think for a moment how a person who acts like himself is accepted at once by everyone he meets. One of the best examples I've ever known is a fellow named Jim Shadday. Jim is a fine person and an effective Christian, and it's a pleasure to be his friend. Jim is a service station attendant, has little higher education, and isn't particularly handsome. He says he enjoys his job because he likes people and this gives him an opportunity to be around them and earn a living at the same time. He has worked at one station for several years.

Jim is the standout in a crowd. He probably never met a man that he didn't like, and he shows it. He makes you feel comfortable around him because he is comfortable around you. Jim has a surplus of enthusiasm, freely shares it with others, and he is as comfortable around a bank president as a beggar. He doesn't try to cover up a lack of education by being stiff and artificial. He can tell you about squirrel hunting with a woodsy relish. Of course, my point is that Jim freely puts his thoughts into words. This should be your aim.

There is no better way to be conversational than to look right into a person's eyes when you are speaking. Too often we look at people without looking into their eyes. You should feel that you're speaking to individuals, not to an audience. When you speak to individual people, you are conversational. I'll have more to say about this later.

Now, while all this is true, your next thought is, "How can I be casual and conversational when I'm scared to death?" It's difficult to be yourself until you learn to live with stage fright.

If you want to learn to speak, you must live with stage fright

Cameron Roach is a vice-president of a rather large bank. He came into one of our classes, making this statement: "I have all the confidence in the world on my job as long as I'm dealing with people I know and with things that I know about. But when it comes to making a talk or doing something that I am not used to doing, I get scared to death."

He went on to explain, "Most people think I am unfriendly, but really I'm just afraid of strange situations." Sound like anybody you know?

In the class Cameron discovered he could train himself to speak and live with stage fright. He found that it took practice and desire. About four months later he told me he had just finished heading a seminar for banking students. He was the chairman and also made speeches. This was an accomplishment he really never thought he could do. He'd never seriously believed he could live with or conquer stage fright to this extent.

Most of us think we are the only person alive who experiences stage fright. Most of us look at a speaker and never detect nervousness or fear, but in reality every speaker has it. And it's just possible that many of the better and highly developed speakers suffer from it more intensely than others. I like the old aphorism that "nervousness is the price a race horse pays for not being a cow." All public speakers learn to live with and enjoy stage fright.

Here are a few facts about this trembling, knee-shaking, mouth-drying, hand-quivering, stomach-churning experience—stage fright.

1. Every speaker experiences it at the beginning of his presentation.
2. It always subsides after a few sentences.
3. It is caused by a fear of failure.
4. Without it your talk would be dull and uninteresting.
5. It helps you do your best by giving your talk emotion and excitement.
6. You'll always have it to some degree.
7. With experience you'll come to appreciate it.

When you get the facts out on the table and discuss them and really understand them, you'll naturally begin to accept this physical phenomenon. When you come to accept it and understand it, you'll begin enjoying it. You can control it, instead of it controlling you.

If you'll only keep your head and assume an outward calm, you can still be badly frightened, yet not let it be known to your audience. Your fear will subside after the first few sentences when you get "all wrapped up" in your topic.

There are also some physical things that you can do to relieve tension. I am told that when you experience stage fright your Adam's apple actually rides up out of its normal position. This tends to restrict your breathing and talking. Swallowing will push it down and allow a more normal passage of air to come and go.

Deep breathing will help calm the butterflies in your stomach. Take three or four deep breaths just before you speak. This'll tranquilize and relax your body.

Sighing will also help you. By this, I mean the pushing out of air through the mouth. This is similar to the effects of yawning, and yawning is what the Creator gave us to relax us naturally.

For your memory, I'll repeat these three physical actions you can do to relax yourself before you make a talk.

1. Swallow several times.
2. Take three or four deep breaths.
3. Sigh or rapidly push out all air from lungs.

Abraham Lincoln never lost his stage fright. He once remarked: "I find speaking here in the House of Representatives and elsewhere about the same thing. I was about as badly scared, and no worse, as I am when I speak in court."

This great speaker stands as an excellent illustration of how interest in your topic will free you from nervousness. Lincoln's biographer, William Herndon, says of him: "At first he was very awkward and it seemed a real labor to adjust himself to his surroundings. He struggled for a time under a feeling of apparent diffidence and sensitiveness . . . as he moved along in his speech he became freer and less uneasy in his movements."

Here was one of our country's greatest public speakers, a President of the United States, who obviously suffered from stage fright. And yet, it has been said of him that when he spoke he was transformed; his eyes kindled, his voice rang, his face shone and seemed to light up the whole assembly.

Lincoln had learned to control stage fright and appreciate it. You can, too! Admit your fears like Lincoln did. Don't pretend to evade fear. Acknowledge it, and this alone will help get rid of it.

Lincoln once said, "I believe I shall never be old enough to speak without embarrassment when I have nothing to talk about." *Knowledge of your subject will give you confidence* that will help overcome stage fright. If you know what you're talking about, and know that you know, you'll be more confident. You are the master of the situation when you know more about your subject than anyone in your audience. This means preparation—apply the seat of your pants to the chair kind. The thrill of doing a good job when speaking will reward you with an inner feeling that you'll seldom experience in other activities. And stage fright makes the victory even sweeter.

If you want to learn to speak, you must cultivate enthusiasm

Eddie Calvert was a computer salesman. One evening while telling of one of his special interests, he explained excitedly how to fertilize properly a Bermuda grass lawn. With a great deal of sparkle and enthusiasm, he detailed what to use and how to do it. He was obviously interested in his subject, and as he spoke he was mentally visualizing his beautiful green lawn.

I looked around the room and noticed that everyone was giving him their best attention. They were sincerely interested in what he was saying.

Now personally, I hate yard work and am sure that there were others in the room who shared my distaste. But if there were, you couldn't tell it. And of course, my point is that everyone in the room, including myself, was excited because Eddie was excited.

Putting enthusiasm into your talk is like sending measles into a schoolroom—it's catching. So, if you want to cultivate enthusiasm for your speaking, put excitement into it. Let your excitement show. I always tell my class members, "If you're as cool as a cucumber, you're probably about as interesting as one."

Enthusiasm always gets its point across and finds listeners. The Duke of Windsor tells about his first attempts at public speaking after he became Prince of Wales: "The more appearances I had to make, the more I came to respect the really first class speech as one of the highest human accomplishments. No one I know seemed to possess that rare degree as Mr. Winston Churchill, who was a sympathetic witness of some of my earlier attempts. 'If you have an important point to make,' he advised, 'don't try to be subtle and clever about it. Use the pile driver. Hit the point once, and then hit it the third time, a tremendous whack.' "

This tremendous whack of enthusiasm always gets your point across. It influences others far more than logic, because logic is cold and void of excitement. Enthusiasm is warm, appealing, and contagious. So then, use it; but when you do, it must be sincere, or it's worse than useless.

Why do you suppose there are more than 250 different religious bodies in the United States alone? Can you explain why anyone can get excited and swept up with Communism or Fascism? How can a handful of radical leaders sway an entire nation? How? Because they are on fire with their beliefs, and they present them with personal conviction—a conviction on which is staked their very existence. This is what William Jennings Bryan meant when he said, ". . . eloquence is thought on fire." It is, and it heats up other people—whether for good or bad.

The early day Christians were no mealy-mouthed, weak-kneed bunch. They played for keeps and they meant business. They had the enthusiasm to preach to the whole world. They influenced others. They persuaded others. They changed others. And you will, too, if you put enthusiasm into your speech.

"There are three things to aim at in public speaking," said Alexander Gregg. "First to get into your subject, then to get your subject into yourself, and lastly, to get your subject into your hearers." All three of these suggestions are accomplished by being excited and enthusiastic—and showing it.

Oh! You say you're just not the enthusiastic type? That you're a more down to earth, stable, plodding type? You say enthusiasm would be unreal and hypocritical for you? Nonsense! Enthusiasm is being sincere, convicted, energetic, and alive. It's not loud yelling, chest pounding, or false show. It's an inner excitement—and it can be cultivated.

Enthusiasm can be cultivated by outward *actions* and by a sincere, positive, and controlled *desire*. Notice these three things that are listed to help you become a more enthusiastic speaker.

1. Make yourself outwardly act excited.
2. Set a speaking goal for yourself.
3. Visualize yourself already a good speaker.

Attitudes and thoughts seem to follow physical action, or to say it another way, *we can change our thinking by changing our actions*. Do you believe this? You should, because you've proved it numerous times. Remember going to the football game the last time? You were thinking about business or how you were going to pay those bills by next Monday, and you were not too excited about the game. But what happened when your team got down on the five yard line and then plunged over for a touchdown? That's right, you completely forgot about reality, jumped to your feet, clenched your fists, and yelled. And how did you feel? Had your mental attitude changed? Sure it had! And all because you made yourself act excited. All because of outward *actions* and circumstances.

Force yourself to act enthusiastically and you'll just naturally adopt that trait. Then in a few days you'll not have to force the actions because they'll become a part of you.

To develop genuine enthusiasm for speaking, you'll need a *goal*, or an *objective*. Make up your mind what you want to do. This can be your intermediate goal—or one that can be reached within one year. Do you want to teach a Sunday school class? Will you have the opportunity to introduce speakers at your civic club or special gathering? What about that next sales meeting or fund drive? What about expressing yourself in the next business meeting at church?

Set a goal for doing any of these things. Write it down and tape it on the inside of your closet door so that you can see it every day. It doesn't have to be rigid, and by all means don't make it so difficult that you'll not reach it. When you've done this, opportunities will usually present themselves to you. If they don't, and you have a goal, you'll make the opportunities.

Before, during, and after your appearances, *visualize yourself as being a good speaker*. This simply means to think of yourself succeeding and feeling the victory. Get in a quiet place, close your eyes, and daydream. Think and picture yourself as you were during your best moments. Feel the audience's attention and appreciation. Feel their applause when you finish. See yourself on the stage of your imagination—standing erect and confident. Your chest is out, your head is up, and you have eye contact with everyone in your audience. They're interested in you and in what you're saying. Feel the words coming out freely, slowly, and with meaning. You're a success, and what's more, you know it.

The visualization can and will have a very important impact on your speaking. So forget your failures and doubts; think only of your past successes. Daydream and picture yourself as already a good speaker, and you'll become one.

Some unknown author has suggested that "intellect may be the throttle of the human machine, the place where control is applied, but emotion is the boiler, the source of all power." This means that enthusiasm touches people—so cultivate it if you want to learn to speak.

Summing-up

You'll want to remember these five things that you must do if you want to learn to speak.

1. You must realize the importance of effective speech.
2. You must have a burning desire.
3. You must be conversational.
4. You must live with stage fright.
5. You must cultivate enthusiasm.

PRACTICE THESE AND PEOPLE WILL LISTEN TO YOU!

Chapter Two

How to choose a topic that's right for you

Andy Andrews was making his best talk thus far in our development course. He forgot himself because he had a message to tell the other men—it was the story about the Prodigal Son. Andy ended his talk with tears in his eyes and said, "This story describes me."

Andy had communicated with the men. No polished orator had ever made a better speech than he did that night. After the class I told him so. He replied, "Oh, I wasn't making a speech; I'm not good at that." He went on to say that he had never been able to get up before people and say anything.

Andy could tell this story with success because he had lived it. He knew what he was talking about. And what's more, he had turned this story over in his mind many dozens of times. It was part of him. Is it any wonder that this talk was a success?

In the same class, just a week before, John Roberts had made a talk and had shown some drawings he had made while in college of pre-stressed concrete beams. John married and became associated with his father in their family grocery store instead of following his college engineering major. He told of stresses, loads, and other things that I didn't understand. Now, how much do you think the class was interested in John's talk about pre-stressed concrete beams? Not much.

On the other hand, if John had told us why a grocery store always keeps its bread at the back, we would have been interested. If he had told us how to save a few cents in our grocery buying each week, we would have listened with eagerness.

Later in the course, John told of applying some human relations principles on his job. He told how much better he was getting along with people as a result of using these principles—increased enthusiasm had made his whole life happier. He told how much more easily he could talk to people and actually be himself. When he expressed these things, he was eloquent. John developed an enthusiasm in speaking because he learned to choose a topic that was right for him. In later weeks he did a great job of holding the interest of his audience.

Why had Andy succeeded with his story? Why had John failed to interest the audience with his talk about pre-stressed concrete beams, but later found success? The answer is so simple that most of us overlook it. We try too hard to choose some big, super-colossal topic and overlook the obvious. *Choosing the right topic is the most important single thing for your speaking success.*

Talk about what you know about

The first principle in choosing a topic that's right for you is: *Talk about what you know about*. This may sound like a cliche, but its importance cannot be overstressed! Andy Andrews wasn't just relating some incidental story, he was describing himself. He had actually lived the story, so he knew something about it. He was talking about what he knew about, and he was a success. Your speaking will be successful if you'll follow this very important principle: Talk about what you know about.

Be interested in it and excited about it

When you have gained the ability to look inside yourself and choose a topic that you know about, there is one other principle that you must apply. This is: *Be interested in it and excited about it.*

You may know all about a topic, but if you aren't interested in it and excited about it, it'll be a flop.

Do you remember the story about Eddie Calvert in the last chapter? When Eddie told about fertilizing his Bermuda grass lawn, he was interested in it and excited about it. See how it fits all of these qualifications?

Each summer my wife sends me out to get rid of the weeds in our lawn. I've had a great deal of experience doing this, so I know how to do it. If I made a talk about pulling weeds, I would know what I was talking about. But obviously it wouldn't be a success, because I'm neither interested in this subject nor excited about it.

Let me repeat the two things that you must remember if your topic is to be a success and one that's right for you.

1. Talk about what you know about.
2. Be interested in it and excited about it.

Remember these things

No speaker or writer produces anything about which he's indifferent. You can't either. *If you're not interested in your subject, you can be sure that no one else will be.* Emotion and interest have to be in your talks. There is no way for them to be successful unless they contain these two ingredients. Speak with your convictions and about them. These are things that will give you strength as a speaker. These are muscle-builders for your talks. With them your talks will be alive and interesting . . . and people will eagerly listen to you.

People identify with people

Jesus knew how to teach people effectively. He used parables or real life examples, and people could see themselves in these stories. When you hear or read of the Prodigal Son, what do you immediately think of? Your relationship with your father or mother? Probably!

Have you ever heard the story of the ten Lepers without placing yourself in their sandals? Even Jesus identified with Lazarus, and was saddened at the occasion of his death, though He knew He would bring him back to life. Among other things Jesus identified with the sorrow of those close to Lazarus.

Like Jesus, you also identify with the lives and sorrows of other people. We call them human interest stories. Nothing will interest your audience more than talking about yourself and about other real people. Use your own experiences as material. Others are interested in what life has taught you. They are interested in your family and friends, your home and hobbies, your joys and sorrows, your ideals and aspirations.

Never, never, never apologize for using a "personal reference," as do many speakers. This is what your audience wants you to use. They want to hear about your life. They want you to be personal. Why is gossip so popular and common? Because it's personal and it involves real people. You can be personal without being vain or egotistical.

Stop, look and listen

While it's true that you should talk about your experiences and interests, you should also constantly seek to broaden these. Become a *noticer*. Notice things around you. Notice people and their interests. Become aware of your surroundings. Ask questions. Stop the rush-rush-rush of life, slow down and look around, and then listen to other people. *Stop* your preoccupation, *look* for details in people and things, and *listen* for new sounds. You'll be amazed at the results of this new approach.

In addition to these things, read as much as possible. Carry a notebook with you at all times.

Reading will broaden your interests as nothing else will. It will also do wonders for your power of concentration and observation. It makes you a much more interesting person.

The notebook habit is a real helper for the success-minded person. This will help you in many areas, but it will be especially helpful in recording ideas for speech topics. Ideas are temporary. Take advantage of them when they come, for they may never reach your conscious mind again.

Summing-up

Let's recap some ideas that you'll want to remember if you're to be successful in choosing a topic that's right for you.

1. Talk about what you know about.
2. Be interested in it and excited about it.
3. People identify with people—Use personal examples and tell about real people.
4. Stop, look and listen—Become aware of your surroundings.

Chapter Three

How to organize your talks

Organization is the shortest distance between two points. A speech without organization is like a voyage without a set destination. Organization is a road-map. It directs your course when speaking. It plots your starting place, your intermediate stops, and your goal or objective. With it you always know where you are and where you're going. Your talk is crippled and loose-jointed without it.

In this chapter I'll tell you how to organize two types of talks. The first will be a short talk; the second will be a longer one. These can be talks to inform or to get action. The short talk might last from one to three minutes. The longer one could be ten to thirty minutes in length. The first one is a condensed version of the longer formula.

Here is the simple one-two-three step formula for organizing a short talk.

   I. Example
  II. Importance
 III. Conclusion

Example is your story, illustration, or the message you want to put across. It's the bulk and meat of your talk. This is your attention getter. By starting immediately with it, you eliminate the old problem of how to get started. This enables you to pack a lot of substance into a short time limit.

Importance is the salesman; it answers the audience's question, "Why should I listen to you?" or "What's in it for me?" This step answers the question that every listener has, "How will I benefit if I do what you want me to do?" It sells the message.

Conclusion wraps up your ideas or clinches the sale. When you've sold your audience, tell them where they can buy your product. Tell them what you want them to do, or tell them what you want them to remember from your talk. Generally you will conclude your talks either one of these two ways:

1. Appeal for action.
2. Summarize the points of your example.

The following is a very clever talk that was delivered one evening by Del Meeks. For your benefit, I have noted the three points of organization.

EXAMPLE

A wealthy industrialist in Pittsburgh had two sons who worked for him in his steel mill. Someday both would inherit all their father's wealth.

The younger son became restless and wanted to get away from the dull, monotonous routine of work and see the world. So, he asked his father to give him all that was now his. The father agreed, and the son was given his share of the wealth.

After receiving his riches, he left Pittsburgh and immediately joined the International Jet Set. He enjoyed the night life in Las Vegas, San Francisco, New York, London, Paris, Rome, and the Riviera. He became known as a real good time Charlie, a real swinger and the last of the big time spenders.

One morning he awoke in a hotel room in Rio de Janeiro and discovered he was broke and destitute. His so-called friends deserted him when they learned of his poverty. Desperate, he took the lowest, most menial employment in order to survive. Finally, he came to his senses and decided that if he was going to have to exist in such a manner, he would go back to his father, ask his forgiveness, and offer to take the lowest job in the steel mill—at least he would be treated fairly and decently.

When he arrived home his father rejoiced at seeing him again. He welcomed him with open arms, purchased new clothes for him, and prepared a big homecoming party to suit the occasion. The son was amazed by his father's love.

Obviously, the story I have just related is a paraphrased version of my favorite Bible story, that of the Prodigal Son, which is found in the fifteenth chapter of Luke. When I read this parable, I visualized it just as I have related it to you—in modern day circumstances.

IMPORTANCE

. . . This parable that our Master related to the Pharisees long ago can be a major source of encouragement to us.

CONCLUSION

. . . It illustrates so vividly God's eagerness to forgive us if we will earnestly repent and seek His forgiveness and mercy.

Del delivered this talk in two minutes. As you see, he didn't waste any time beginning. He didn't apologize or warm-up. He simply began his talk by beginning his story. It caught the immediate attention of the audience. When he told his story he then nailed it down, or sold it, by explaining the benefits (encouragement). Finally, he concluded by recommending that we repent and seek God's forgiveness and mercy.

This type of story is very difficult to put over in a first class manner, but Del did a perfect job of presenting it. It was a talk that I shall never forget. Can you see this talk succeeding without organization?

Below is listed a four point formula for organizing a longer talk.

   I. Attention
  II. Importance
 III. Examples
 IV. Conclusion

To help you remember this formula, visualize and remember this short story.

A top sergeant strides in front of his men and yells: "ATTENTION! All right men, it's IMPORTANT that each one of you be a good EXAMPLE of a soldier today, because this CONCLUDES boot camp, and tomorrow we ship out."

Now that you have read and will remember this story, let's go on to a larger outline of this formula.

  I. ATTENTION
    A. Statement of fact.
    B. Unusual anecdote.
    C. Strong example.
    D. Authoritative quotation.
    E. Arresting question.
  II. IMPORTANCE
    A. Why should the audience be interested?
    B. How will this help them?

III. EXAMPLES
   A. Stories relative to topic or theme.
   B. Proves or lends weight to topic or theme.
   C. Be specific with names, dates and places.
IV. CONCLUSION
   A. Appeal for action, (or)
   B. Summarize points.

The difference in this formula and the one for a shorter talk is obvious. In a short talk you usually don't have time for an attention step, so you let your example get your audience's attention. In this formula, we take our time and let each part mesh into the whole.

I'll probably never forget how one man used an arresting question to gain attention. In making a talk on the creation of man, Gene Whitney started it by asking, "Did Adam have a navel?" I don't remember the exact content of his talk, but I'll never forget that lead. And did he ever get the attention of his audience!

We must realize that in a longer talk from ten to thirty minutes, we usually have to rekindle the interest of the audience several times. This is accomplished by each of these steps, and by using several good examples.

Now, let's look and see how a well-known speaker followed this same outline. This is Paul's speech on Mars Hill as recorded in Acts 17:22-31.

ATTENTION

Ye men of Athens, I perceive that in all things ye are too

superstitious. For as I passed by, and beheld your devotions, I found an altar with this inscription, TO THE UNKNOWN GOD.

IMPORTANCE

Whom therefore ye ignorantly worship, him declare I unto you.

EXAMPLES

God that made the world and all things therein, seeing that He is Lord of heaven and earth, dwelleth not in temples made with hands; Neither is worshipped with men's hands, as though he needed anything, seeing he giveth to all life, and breath, and all things; And hath made of one blood all nations of men for to dwell on all the face of the earth, and hath determined the times before appointed, and the bounds of their habitation; That they should seek the Lord, if haply they might feel after him, and find him, though he be not far from everyone of us: For in him we live, and move, and have our being; as certain also of your own poets have said, For we are also his offspring. Forasmuch then as we are the offspring of God, we ought not to think that the Godhead is like unto gold or silver or stone, graven by art and man's device.

CONCLUSION

And the times of this ignorance God winked at; but now commandeth all men everywhere to repent; Because he hath appointed a day, in which he will judge the world in righteousness by that man whom he hath ordained; whereof he hath given assurance unto all men, in that he hath raised him from the dead.

Do you see the order and organization of this speech? Paul did a masterful job of gaining attention, selling its importance, saying his message, and then concluding it. Without proper organization, your talks are just a bundle of loose ends. Tie them together with thought and order. Use these two simple formulas for organizing talks. When you do, you'll find that your speaking will take on a new dimension of *effectiveness, confidence,* and *acceptance.*

Summing-up

Organization directs your course while you're speaking. It plots your starting place, your intermediate stops, and your goal or objective. With it you know where you are and where you're going.

In this chapter you learned how to organize:

1. A short talk
2. A longer talk

You also learned how to begin and end a talk. Remember these suggestions and come back to them frequently.

Chapter Four

How
to practice
your talk

Several years ago Don Williamson, a minister friend, visited in our home until quite late in the evening. We were deeply involved in some church-related discussion.

The next day was Wednesday and Don brought the sermon that night. And you know what? It was exactly a retread of what we had discussed the night before! And more important, it was delivered with tremendous conviction and interest. He had a message, which was well delivered and forcefully presented.

After the service was over, I remarked to him about his lengthy preparation and asked, "Why do you ever need to study when you have friends like us to help you?" I received a grin. It was years later that I realized what had actually happened.

Whether he took his sermon from our conversation, or purposely started the conversation in order to practice his sermon—who knows now. The important thing is that he had practiced his sermon in private conversation. He found what struck a bell with us. Our conversation stimulated his thinking, and this gave him new insights. By using this method of practicing the talk, he was able to weed out the unrelated and uninteresting material.

I remember reading how Bob Hope's writers test-run their jokes on each other before they use them. Then Mr. Hope gets them, studies them for emphasis, rolls them around orally for awhile, and finally tests them on his writers.

From this series of tests, it is decided if a joke will stand or not. If the writers aren't broken up, the joke is thrown out. Hours are spent on the quips to be sure the punchline and timing are done correctly. But when Mr. Hope steps before the camera you'd think each one was spontaneous and natural.

Much has been said about the Gettysburg Address. Some say Mr. Lincoln delivered it after only a few hours, preparation. Some say that while he was on the train, he jotted a few ideas down on the back of an envelope to use for notes. However, other historians claim that over half of this material was presented in an earlier speech. They say he took this material and combined it with other thoughts to form the now famous address. This is probably true.

These were the thoughts he had while discussing the painful problems of war with the other government officials. This address reveals the problems that gnawed at him during those sleepless nights. There's no telling how many times he had actually practiced this talk in private conversation and thoughts. When you consider all this, plus his emotional involvement, no wonder it has gone down in history as the greatest American classic.

Now contrast all this with a person standing in front of a mirror practicing his speech. He is conscious of his smile, which is forced and artificial, his right arm is swooping down and out like a student conductor of a junior high orchestra. This person is so interested in his outward appearance that he will likely forget his message. Remember this, if you remember nothing else in this whole book: *good speakers get so engrossed in their message, topic, or subject that they forget their outward effects.*

Interest and conviction make a talk, not

beautiful gestures. Emotional enthusiasm and strong inner feelings produce good gestures and facial expressions. Don't practice your smile and gestures; get busy and *strengthen your interest and conviction* about your subject. Become embroiled in it. Let it become a part of you.

One of the most eloquent speakers I have ever heard was a little fellow named Roby Fletcher. You wouldn't pick Roby as a stand-out in a crowd, and he never considered himself an eloquent speaker. You would have to strain to hear him, and his English could be improved some, but when he made the following talk it hammered an impact on me that I shall never forget. Here's what he said:

Not long ago, things were really going against us. I lost my job and couldn't seem to find another one anywhere. Our money ran out, and then our food was gone. There we were—we had no food in the house and there was absolutely no money to buy anything to eat. Not only did we have this problem, but our rent was due and most of our bills were two months behind. What would we do? What would happen to us?

I felt like I was inside a pressure cooker. I worried so much that I had trouble breathing. I'd go to bed at night and lay there awake until 3:00 or 4:00 in the morning. This went on for weeks. When the sun came up, it was just another useless day; when it went down, it meant the coming of another sleepless night.

One day, while I was sitting at home worrying, I said to my wife, "This won't work. If this is all there is to life, I don't want any more of it."

My prayers had been shallow and without much conviction. My wife and I discussed the situation, and she suggested that both of us pray more fervently and really believe that God would help us.

We began doing just this and things started to change. Each day something would go right for us. Somehow we managed to have just enough food for that day. We wouldn't know where it would come from, but the same thing would happen the next day also. Odd jobs started coming to me. The first one lasted only three hours. After that came two or three days of work, and soon it multiplied into a full time job.

We continued to pray and we continued to eat. Gradually our bills were paid. This has truly taught me the value of prayer.

Can you see Roby standing up before a mirror practicing his facial expressions, voice, body gestures, and pauses? Of course not! He had practiced this talk many times in conversation with his wife and in his own personal thoughts. It had so welled up inside of him that when he talked it flowed out with such eloquence that there was not a dry eye in the whole room. And his gestures, voice inflections, pauses, and eye contact were as perfect as any person's who has ever spoken publicly.

Do like Roby did: *practice your talk by becoming convinced about your subject*, or by picking a subject about which you are already convinced.

Give your talk a test flight

After an airplane has had repairs, the chief mechanic and pilot will usually take it up for a test flight to see if it is air-worthy. Why don't you do the same thing and *give your talks a test flight?* You can do this around the breakfast table or during a coffee break or to the man next to you in the plant.

If you're going to make a talk on your favorite hobby, simply turn to one of these people and say, "You know what I like about golf? I can really relax and get away from everything. Yesterday we were on the eighth green and . . ."

When you're giving your talk a test flight, check for points of interest in the other person and you'll quickly see what to keep and what to leave out. Oh, you say you don't have time to do this type of practicing? Come now, wasn't it just last week, as you were reading the morning paper at the breakfast table, that your wife remarked, "I wish you'd talk to me instead of reading that paper every morning." Or was it just yesterday?

Give your talks a test flight; test their effectiveness on other people.

Practice without pressure

The story has been told many times about how Ben Hogan practiced hitting his golf shots. Someone said he practiced every shot hundreds of times in his imagination. He imagined the hole to be as big as a washtub. He visualized his swing and imagined the ball going right into the cup.

I have read that an average weekend golfer can

take seven or eight strokes off his game by proper imagination and visualization. The secret is to practice without pressure. This means to get in a quiet place, without distractions, and mentally visualize yourself hitting the ball. This programs your computer for accurate delivery. When you swing the club, you don't think about your back-swing or your follow-through, you think about the ball; your subconscious computer goes into operation as it has been programmed.

Now, let's apply all this to your speaking. Get in a quiet place where there's no noise or distractions. *Picture yourself behind that rostrum and visualize yourself standing calm and confident.* You are in control of the situation and you know it. Your words are coming freely. You are speaking slowly, and as soon as you're ready for a new thought or word it comes to you. You're not hurried. The audience is completely with you; you have their best attention. You're looking directly into the eyes of the people; they're giving you approval, and this is more fuel for your confidence. Your message is sinking into their minds and they are nodding their approval and interest. You're succeeding and it feels great.

As you program these things into your mental environment, they will become a part of you and you'll actually adopt these attitudes into your subconscious mind. This will help you strengthen your speaking goals. Practice without pressure. It'll do great things for you.

Psychologists tell us that we *learn fast* under crisis situations, but we don't *learn well*. This simply means that the child who was thrown into the creek and had to learn to swim in a crisis situation didn't learn to swim well and probably will never be a really good swimmer. Tests have been made on rats that were permitted to learn a set course in a maze without any pressure on them. Their learning was slower in some cases, but their later performance was superior to rats who learned in a crisis situation. Enough tests and studies have been made to show that if you learn without pressure, you'll hold up better under stress.

Keep your eye on the ball

Before you speak and while you speak, keep the purpose of your talk before you. Concentrate on what you are there for and what you want the audience to gain from your talk. When you do this, you are emulating professional golfers —you're keeping your eye on the ball. Don't worry about your backswing—concentrate on the ball. Don't worry about your outward actions—think about your message. The moment you really learn this concept you'll immediately become a successful speaker.

Summing-up

I'd like for you to remember that interest and

conviction make a talk successful, not outward effects. *Good speakers get engrossed in their message.* Don't be overly concerned with how you're going to look, but concern yourself with how well you and your message are tied together.

These three suggestions will permit you to practice your talk in a natural and effective way.

1. Give your talk a test flight—tell it in a casual way to your wife or friend.

2. Practice without pressure—vividly imagine yourself succeeding as a speaker.

3. Keep your eye on the ball—keep your purpose before you.

Chapter Five

How to read scripture so your audience will understand it

About one hundred years after the death of Christ, Justin Martyr indicates that the common practice of public Scripture reading was well-known and firmly established as a chief part of worship services.

As the centuries passed this changed. In the Dark Ages the Bible was kept from the people. Today, Scripture reading usually occupies a small part, if any, of our worship services. Why?

Well, there are several reasons: one is that so many times the reader does a very ineffective job. He doesn't really convey a proper understanding. People don't understand what is being read; thus, the Word of God is limited.

To be effective, Scripture reading must be understood. This may be an over-simplification, but how many times have you had someone stand and read a selection when you didn't know what he was reading about or who was speaking? How often does the audience really understand?

Please notice this reading from Nehemiah 8:4, 6, 8:

And Ezra the scribe stood upon a pulpit of wood, which they had made for the purpose . . . And Ezra opened the book in the sight of all the people; (for he was above all the people); and when he opened it all the people stood . . . They read from the book in the law of God, distinctly, and gave the sense, and caused them to understand the reading.

Notice these three things about this reading:

1. Ezra read from the law of God clearly.
2. The Levites explained the reading.
3. The people understood it.

Read, explain, and understand—these are the key points.

But then, you already know these things, as you have made these observations yourself. So, let's discuss two elements of proper reading.

Effective Scripture reading consists of two

things: *preparation* and *presentation*. Preparation is private and presentation is public. Preparation is the cause and presentation is the effect. They are two halves; one isn't complete without the other. Preparation is what no one sees but is quite visible in the presentation.

I asked our minister, Joe Barnett, how he mentally prepared for a Scripture reading. He said, "I think a careful personal experience with the Scripture to be read, coupled with fervent prayer for direction in doing an effective job, are the two essential ingredients for mental preparation for public reading of the Scriptures."

He went on to say, "I make mental preparation by a careful personal reading of the passage, or passages, involved in an attempt to find their message for me. I find it impossible to read the Scriptures adequately to others without first seeking a message for my personal needs. I feel that if I can get myself in a mental state whereby the Scripture really says something to me, I have a greater desire to put it over to others.

"I never read a Scripture passage in public without first praying to God for direction, that He will cleanse my own life so that I might be more worthy of reading His Holy Word to others."

These ideas will help you in your mental preparation. In addition, there are some things you'll want to do to physically prepare yourself for an effective job of Scripture reading. You'll certainly want to read enough of the context so that you know the setting and what the passage really says. I like to underline words that I feel should be stressed. This helps me to put emphasis into the reading and gets rid of monotony. You should know the proper pronunciation of each word.

After these things have been done, you'll want actually to read the Scripture aloud several times. Words frequently sound different when read aloud. You need to get the feel of the words, especially if you're reading from the King James Version. Be sure you can say the "thees" and "thous" and "didsts" without getting tied up. By doing this, you become familiar with the word sounds and the meanings. Don't stand in front of a mirror and practice your gestures. Don't be concerned with outward effects when practicing—do be concerned with *understanding the message*.

After you have thoroughly prepared and are familiar with the passages, here are four suggestions that will help make your presentation effective:

1. Introduce speaker, persons spoken to, and context.
2. Concentrate on the message and feeling of writer.
3. Communicate with the audience.
4. Speak slowly and distinctly.

The above suggestions are listed in order of importance. The most important item is a proper introduction. This means to set the stage, or to *put the audience into a proper mental environment*. When you do this, you promote proper understanding. This can be accomplished in one or two simple sentences just before you start reading. Identify the writer or speaker, indicate to whom he is writing, and in just a few words describe the context.

Then when you begin reading, every word will have meaning to the audience. Can't you see how important it is for the audience to be able to identify the writer or speaker, to whom he is speaking, and what is he speaking about before they can possibly understand the reading?

The next idea that will promote effectiveness and understanding is to concentrate on the message and feeling of the writer. This will not only help you forget yourself, but it will add emphasis to your reading. The worst thing you can do is to be conscious of yourself—if you're smiling, if your hair is combed, if your shoulders are squared, or if your voice is pitched just right.

If you are really concentrating on the message and feeling of the writer, your outward effects will be right. So don't worry about them, but get yourself emotionally involved in your message. The most successful readers are the persons who call least attention to themselves. The audience is thinking about the message instead of the man.

You have prepared so well that the last two

things come naturally and without much thought. You communicate with your audience by looking at them occasionally, thus including them in the reading. Speak slowly, distinctly, and with conviction, thereby emphasizing the importance of the message and your desire that it be understood.

These last two things are effects that are produced by certain causes. The causes are *prayer, proper preparation*, and a *feeling* for the message. Don't try to attack these effects directly, but work on the causes and the effects will come naturally.

Here is a sample of an introduction to a Scripture that I read recently:

In the 4th chapter of Genesis, Moses records these things for our knowledge: the first family, the birth of Cain and Abel, the first murder, and, in the 9th verse, God's confronting Cain with his sin.

"Then the Lord said to Cain . . ."

Notice that I attempted to set the stage with a brief introduction of the speaker or writer (Moses), persons spoken to (us or future generations), and the context (first family, Cain and Abel, first murder, and God's confronting Cain).

Let's suppose you are to read from Ephesians 6. You might begin your reading with an introduction like this:

> The apostle Paul writes to the church that he started in Ephesus and in Chapter 6 instructs them as to their Christian duties. He is writing to children and parents, servants and masters. "Children, obey your parents in the Lord . . ."

I hope this gives you some relevant suggestions and not abstract platitudes. These suggestions aren't meant to be mechanical. They are a check list in your preparation. Don't concern yourself with the method but give attention to the message, and you'll become skilled at Scripture reading. Begin and end your preparation with prayer.

Mentally picture a person with a strong personal communion with God. His words and his character are mingled so that they are inseparable. He communicates God's message because he understands it and reveres it. He calls attention to its meaning instead of to himself. The audience is more aware of the message than they are of the man. And as Nehemiah suggests, he reads from the law of God clearly so that the people understand the reading. And when the people understand, the reading has been successful.

Summing-up

To be effective, Scripture reading must be understood. This involves two separate areas:

Preparation and *Presentation*. Proper preparation means to get to know the reading, its context, its theme, and purpose. Proper presentation starts with setting the stage, or introducing the reading.

When you're reading in public, these four suggestions will help you:

1. Introduce speaker, persons spoken to, and context.
2. Concentrate on the message and feeling of writer.
3. Communicate with the audience.
4. Speak slowly and distinctly.

Good, effective Scripture reading is caused by prayer, proper preparation, and a feeling for the message—work on the *causes* and the *effects* will come naturally.

Chapter Six

How to introduce a speaker in a brief and effective way

The purpose of this chapter is to explain an effective way to introduce a speaker—a way that makes both him and the audience feel important.

Nothing is more butchered, not even the King's English, than most speeches of introduction. Across the land in thousands of places—at luncheons and dinners, churches and clubs —hundreds of speakers are murdered by poor introductions. It's true that no court will sentence the offenders, but their audiences will. And what's more, it's the poor victim who takes the rap.

Recently, I served as president of the Amarillo Exchange Club. During this time I took careful notice of the way program chairmen introduced speakers. I noticed the influence that introductions had on speakers and audiences, and during the entire year I only heard three or four good introductions. As a rule, church gatherings are usually no better. The introductions are usually long and disorganized.

When we hear an introducer start off by saying, "Our speaker needs no introduction . . . ," we immediately know that the poor fellow isn't going to get one—at least not one that's effective and enthusiastic.

Anything that calls attention to the introducer is bad taste. One of the most glaring things that calls attention to himself is his lack of confidence in giving the introduction. Usually he looks down at the floor and doesn't speak clearly. Words drop right off his chin and hit the floor with a dull thud.

Another way in which the introducer can call attention to himself is by using too many personal pronouns. One or two will be forgiven but no more. You are selling the speaker, not yourself. Some introducers are guilty of telling about personal experiences—this is in bad taste as well as being time consuming. This will be a greater temptation when the speaker and the introducer are close friends. Just stick to the facts—the facts about the speaker, that is.

Over a period of time I've noticed several common faults made by those who introduce speakers. I'll list these faults and then discuss them. Our purpose is to learn what *motivates* the audience and the speaker, and what *misses* the mark. We'll better understand the importance of making the speaker feel *important*, and at the same time arouse the *interest* of the audience. We'll call these:

SIX WAYS TO MURDER A SPEAKER

1. Steal his time by making a speech yourself.
2. Toss flowery bouquets instead of simple, specific truths.
3. Show off your knowledge of his subject.
4. Show no enthusiasm for his subject.
5. Use stale phrases.
6. Summarize his talk after he has finished speaking.

1. *Steal his time by making a speech yourself.* Most introductory speeches can be effectively given in 30 seconds. A few may take as long as a minute, but these are rare exceptions. The chairman should realize that the audience has gathered, not to hear him, but to hear the speaker.

2. *Toss flowery bouquets instead of simple,*

specific truths. Many people think that the best way to introduce a speaker is to "sugar coat" him, or to heap as many bouquets as possible on him. Usually, this is embarrassing to the speaker because he knows he cannot possibly live up to the billing. Expressing appreciation and mentioning actual good accomplishments are fine, but flowers smell too sweet. Often the introducer tries to identify with the speaker and even tosses a few bouquets at himself indirectly (he thinks). *Exaggerated compliments offend most audiences and embarrass most speakers.* So be sincere and stick to the simple, specific truths.

3. *Show off your knowledge of his subject.* Here's one that you've probably heard before—if not in actual content, you've heard its equal.

It goes like this: "Today we're going to hear a talk and see some slides about the Holy Land. I know that each and every one of you will enjoy it because I was there three years ago and really enjoyed it. Incidentally, I'll have to bring my slides and show them sometime! I'll never forget how sick I got from drinking the water . . ."

You'll never know exactly what is going through the speaker's mind, but you can be certain of one thing—he'll wish the introducer was in the Holy Land—NOW.

4. *Show no enthusiasm for his subject.* Professional speakers live in horror of being introduced by this type of person. He usually sets

the stage for a nice long nap. A speaker must possess the wit of Will Rogers and the volume of William Jennings Bryan to overcome this mood. Enthusiasm breeds enthusiasm. It sets the pace for the speaker's performance and the listeners' attitudes.

5. *Use stale phrases.* Closely akin to the last butchering device is the one of using stale or moldy phrases. For instance, "Our speaker needs no introduction," "Ladies and gentlemen, it's indeed a rare privilege for me to introduce . . ." Have you ever noticed that the speaker is always an "expert in his field"? With some people everything is a "great and glorious honor." Watch these. Be simple and specific—and alive.

6. *Summarize his talk after he has finished speaking.* The last meat-cleaver is the fellow who won't quit with a simple "thank you," but who has to do a little preaching and summarizing when the speaker sits down. This shows bad manners and poor taste. It steals the spotlight from the speaker—who justly deserves the recognition and appreciation.

The above six suggestions are negative and are listed this way for emphasis. They suggest what you *shouldn't do.* The remainder of this chapter will deal with what you *should do,* or how to do an effective job of introducing a speaker. A formula and some examples are given. We're concerned with getting the speaker off the starting blocks with a fast start, and on the right foot.

A good way to accomplish these purposes is to answer the following four questions—questions that listeners always silently ask.

How to organize a speech of introduction

    I. SUBJECT (what is the subject?)
   II. BENEFITS (What will I get out of it?)
  III. QUALIFICATIONS (What are the speaker's qualifications?)
  IV. NAME (What is the speaker's name?)

It's always a problem to begin. If we have a simple and sound beginning, we usually carry through just fine. The easiest and simplest way to begin an introduction is to say, "The subject that we'll hear today is __ __ _____."

The next question that the audience wants answered is, "How is this going to help me?" or "What am I going to get out of it?" So tell them how they'll benefit. The talk has some purpose. It may be to educate, inspire, or entertain. Whatever it is, be specific and plainly tell them how it will help them. This is a most important item in motivating the audience to listen and be interested. It sells the subject.

The third question that you'll want to answer is, "What are the speaker's qualifications?" Does he have a degree? Is he the leading salesman? Has he been a minister—how long and in what city? What qualifies him to be speaking on this subject? These are the things the audience wants to know. Mention from two to four specific qualifications. These aren't opinions, accolades, or flowers, but simple facts.

Finally, "What is the speaker's name?" The most effective way that I've ever heard is to finish the third point, pause two or three seconds—the pause has the power of a sledge hammer—then with firmness and slightly increased volume state the speaker's name. When you increase your volume as you pronounce his name, you are giving a verbal fanfare to the speaker, and this is impressive—as well as stimulating. It creates excitement and enthusiasm in both the audience and the speaker.

Here are two introductions that come to my mind. These are some that I have given. Notice the simple organization.

SUBJECT

Today we'll have a program entitled "Egypt—Ancient and Modern" . . .

BENEFITS

You'll find this to be interesting as well as educational, and you'll recognize its historical significance.

QUALIFICATIONS

Our speaker has made a recent trip to Europe, the Holy Lands, and Egypt. He is a professor of Bible at Harding College in Searcy, Arkansas. He is currently speaking each evening at the Fair Park Coliseum.

NAME

(pause)—Jimmy Allen!

This introduction lasted only 30 to 35 seconds. It fit all four parts of the outline. Here's another sample:

SUBJECT

Your program this morning is, "The Concept of Freedom."

BENEFITS

It will remind us of our national heritage and reinforce us against the modern slogans of "God is Dead," and "Better Red than Dead!"

QUALIFICATIONS

Our speaker has been in the newspaper business for 43 years. He is the editor of the Amarillo Daily News. He is vitally interested in Americanism.

NAME

(Pause)—Wes Izzard.

So here you have it! A brief, enthusiastic, and effective way to introduce a speaker. You can apply it at your next sales meeting, church gathering, or civic club. With its application you'll *help the audience feel excited and important;* and more than that, you'll *give the speaker a nice shot of enthusiasm.*

Summing-up

Follow this simple, four-part outline and you'll answer the important questions that every audience silently asks:

1. SUBJECT (What is the subject?)
2. BENEFITS (What will I get out of it?)
3. QUALIFICATIONS (What are the speaker's qualifications?)
4. NAME (What is the speaker's name?)

The best way to begin is to say simply, "The subject that we'll hear today is ___ ___ ___ ___."

The best way to end is to finish with the speaker's qualifications, pause two or three seconds, and state the speaker's name.

Try these things and you'll immediately be one of the rare few who make the speaker feel important. You'll also raise the enthusiasm level of the audience.

Chapter Seven

Some do's and don'ts

Your effectiveness as a speaker is measured by the way people listen to you and how they remember what you say. If your audience understands you, they will remember you more—the degree of their remembering determines the degree of your success. Psychologists tell us that an audience will usually forget about 95% of what they hear, retaining only 5%. By any measurement, this is a poor success story.

With this in mind, your next question is, "What can I do to make people remember what I have to say?" In asking this, you've hit the question that every speaker should keep before him at all times.

Is there anything that you can do to improve the impact of your words? Yes, there is! And it is the purpose of this chapter to go over some handy helps for you. So let's get down to brass tacks and talk about the first suggestion that will help you speak so people will listen to you.

Do use simple and specific words

Demosthenes is remembered for his oratory and ivory-tower speaking, but you are remembered when you use simple and specific words and terms. This famous Greek orator and statesman lived three hundred years before Christ, and life was slower then. His audience had time to spend their days listening to new ideas. This gave way to the development of style and artificial, pompous speaking. Today, people are in a hurry; they want it quick and simple. More people read the *Reader's Digest* than Homer's *Iliad*.

You and I use simple and specific words in our everyday conversations because they convey a quick and clear meaning. But when many speakers mount the platform they change from a casual manner to a stiff and artificial one.

1. *What are Simple Words?* They are words that are personal and intimate—they're the stuff that our conversation is loaded with. Simple words strike quick meanings in your listeners' minds. Simple words cannot be broken down into smaller parts.

Specific words—ones that immediately stick in the listener's mind—are such descriptive words as Uncle George, Aunt Susie, Cousin Clarence, Doctor Jones, etc. When we say *you* or *yours* we are specific and direct. *Me, us, our* are good words to use because they're personal, and all audiences like to be included in personal conversation. Nothing adds more realism and interest to a talk than actual names. This is why personal references or endorsements are so common and effective in advertising and selling. When a well-known football pro endorses a cereal, kids want to try it; not because it has niacin, thiamine, and iron in it.

Simple words are familiar words. I remember reading a book recently that was filled with long, complex words. I referred to a dictionary three or four times on each page, and could hardly retain my train of thought. This would be considered scholarly by some, but it was tedious and boring to me.

When you read or hear someone speak, you don't want to stop, think, and translate too often. Simple and specific words paint pictures in your mind. Your mind is filled with *thoughts*, instead of getting hung on *hard words*.

2. *Use Active Verbs.* Active verbs help make your speech simple and specific. Prefer the clear verb to the flowery adjective and people will understand you. Active verbs give your speech a simple style—one that's easy to follow. Here are some examples of using active verbs:

> The blacksmith's hammer *rang* the anvil.
> The dog *snarled* at the postman.
> The rain's *pouring*; let's *dash* to the car.
> The test pilot *crash-landed* the plane.
> The golfer *exploded* the ball out of the sand trap.

Clear, active verbs tell a story and create thoughts in your listeners' minds without calling attention to your style or to themselves. Of course, adjectives are important but can be overdone when they are rose-colored, sugar-coated, and ivory-towered.

3. *Is a Preposition Something You Should Never End a Sentence With?* Why not end a sentence with a preposition? People do it every day in their conversation. Occasionally a preposition is a very descriptive way to end a sentence. Often it seems natural, conversational, and informal. I've heard some stuffed shirt speakers whom I've hoped would end a sentence with a preposition just to prove they were human after all.

Here are the ten most used prepositions in our language today:

at   in   to   from   like
for   of   at   on   with

Once when Winston Churchill was Prime Minister, he was criticized by a young intellectual for ending a sentence with a preposition. Churchill scribbled a note to the man, which in essence said, "This is the sort of nonsense up with which I will not put."

So who does the critic consider an authority on grammar? Shakespeare? Did he stoop to ending any sentence with prepositions? Sure, he did! Hundreds of times. Here are just a couple of examples from his famous Hamlet's soliloquy:

The heart-ache and the thousand natural shocks that flesh is heir to . . .
And makes us rather bear those ills we have, than fly to others that we know not of?

4. *Use Plenty of Contractions.* Contractions help make your speaking informal and effective. They are used every day in conversation. They're natural and they save time. Contractions are words like:

I'll	you've	he's	she'll	it's
we're	they're	aren't	isn't	haven't
won't	shouldn't	can't	don't	doesn't
didn't	here's	let's	what's	

When you call your child, she doesn't say, "*I will* be there in a minute." She says, "*I'll* be there . . ." Can you imagine the old expression, "*He'll* do it every time" changed to, "*He will* do it every time"? And you can think of many others to prove this point.

Of course, there are exceptions to the above rule. When you want to add emphasis to a statement, you might say, "I will not!" And then your wife might answer, "Yes, you will!"

However, there are some instances where contractions just do not sound right—especially when you want to emphasize them. If they don't sound right, don't use them.

The general use of contractions will help your speaking reach a more informal tone—use them often.

5. *Don't Be Afraid Of Repetition.* One of the old rules of public speaking is:

a. Tell 'em what you're going to tell 'em.
b. Then tell 'em.
c. And then tell 'em what you've told 'em.

Another suggestion is to take a simple point and tell it in three stories. Don't shy away from repeating a word or a thought. People remember what you say longer when you use effective repetition.

Jesus was a master at this. Notice how effectively He used repetition as a teaching device. This is told in Matthew 13:44-49.

Again, the kingdom of heaven is like unto treasure hid in a field; the which when a man hath found, he hideth, and for joy thereof goeth and selleth all that he hath, and buyeth that field.

Again, the kingdom of heaven is like unto a merchant man, seeking goodly pearls: Who when he had found one pearl of great price, went and sold all that he had, and bought it.

Again, the kingdom of heaven is like unto a net, that was cast into the sea, and gathered of every kind: Which when it was full, they drew to shore, and sat down, and gathered the good into vessels, but cast the bad away.

So shall it be at the end of the world: the angels shall come forth, and sever the wicked from among the just.

See how Christ used repetition with the three "agains" and three illustrations to put across His point? Then He concluded by telling them again.

One reason we remember the poems of Rudyard Kipling is because he used repetition so well. Remember, from your school years, these two lines?

"What are the bugles blowing for?" said Files-on-Parade.
"To turn you out, to turn you out," the Colour-Sergeant said.

Or how about this one from Kipling's poem, *Mother O'Mine*. Remember it?

If I were hanged on the highest hill,
Mother o'mine, O mother o'mine!
I know whose love would follow me still,
Mother o'mine, O mother o'mine!

There are many ways to use effective repetition in our speaking. We use them all the time in our conversation, although we aren't aware of it so much. So think about it some; you'll find it'll help you speak so people will listen to you. It'll also help you use simple and specific words.

Don't be pompous and trite

A pompous speaker is full of fluff and generalities. He's pretentious and artificial—the guy that you don't enjoy. He may be sold on his own importance, or he may be a speaker who laughs at his own dull jokes. He may look down his nose at you, or be too bookish and dusty.

Here is a clever speech that was delivered at a Rotary Club meeting by a good friend of mine, Bob Haynes. This was done in humor, but you've probably heard someone deliver similar talks—ones that weren't meant to be funny.

My fellow citizens and countrymen everywhere in the world:

It is with a deep sense of responsibility and profound humility that I stand before you today.

There are many burning issues facing us today—inflation, war, crime, immorality; and it is on this topic I wish to direct your attention.

All through American history one point has stood out indelibly clear for everyone to see—a point about which there was no doubt in the mind of any. Be he friend, foe, or pacifist.

Now, my friends, I ask you, "Can you continue to let the ship of state drift—drift through these perilous waters?" For drifting can only mean one thing. And that is wreckage on the treacherous rocks of indifference and apathy. For we cannot long endure the onslaught of this ignominious assassin of national character. We must join arms and close ranks so as to provide an impenetrable united front which will endure.

As I look out upon your eager faces, I do not wish to unduly excite or alarm you, for there is a solution. A solution which will serve us well, just as it has served our founding fathers—Washington, Jefferson, Lincoln, and Roosevelt.

What is the solution? It is simple equity! Yes, equity! What is equity? Is equity equality, freedom, liberty, or is it on a broader and nobler plane—magnanimity? While some may say it is none of these, I say that in one sense it may be all of these.

What is our course then? The way appears clear. To pursue that unbending and inflexible course which down through the ages of time has so loyally supported each who has espoused its course. With our goal clearly in mind and our sleeves rolled up—working back to back—we shall in that final day achieve our ultimate aim . . .

Lincoln once remarked about a fellow lawyer, "That man can cram more words into fewer thoughts than anyone I've ever known." And today many speakers imitate this lawyer friend of Lincoln.

Here are a few things that you, as a speaker, shouldn't do. We'll discuss them in the negative form. They're enemies of clear, lucid speech. They make you pompous and trite.

1. *Don't Refer To Yourself As "We."* I remember a children's story that involved a little boy. At the breakfast table he'd say, "We want

cereal for breakfast." After breakfast he asked his mother, "May we go outside?" All day, it was "we" this and "we" that. Because he had a frog in his pocket!

Now, every time I hear someone say "we," instead of "I" or "me," I usually think of the little boy with the frog. And I always want to jump up and say: "What's a matter, ya gotta frog in yer pocket?"

If a speaker is humble and isn't trying to brag or boast, what's wrong with his saying "I" or "me"? You wouldn't say, "We must go now and mow our grass," in private conversation. So why do we do it in public speaking?

2. *Don't Use Long, Difficult Words Too Often.* Simple words are words that cannot be broken down into smaller parts. Complex words are ones that have either prefixes or suffixes. Prefixes are added to the front of words to change their meaning. As an example, the *re* in *redeem*, or the *tri* in *triangle*. A suffix adds to the meaning of a word by placing another syllable at the ending of the word. As an example, the *ade* in *lemonade*, or the *let* in *booklet*.

Our minds recognize and understand many of these complex words upon hearing them, without thinking or having to stop and analyze them. However, there are many we hear that we have to stop and think just what the meaning is and how it affects the context of the speaker's message. When this happens, our minds are momentarily distracted and we miss much of the speaker's message.

You don't have to be a student of grammar to see how much more the human brain can program, compute, and digest when each word gives a clear picture. So let this be one of your traits in speaking—narrow the complex words down to simple ones and you'll find that people are *listening* more and *understanding* you better.

3. *How To Use Slang.* Some people ask, "Should slang ever be used in public speaking?" The answer is, "Of course! If it's done in the proper setting, with the right audience." You'd probably want to shy away from it if you were addressing the Grandmothers' China Painting Convention, but if you were the speaker at a youth meeting, you'd be obliged to use slang—provided it was current and in style.

Slang changes often. You'd better know the current meaning of your words or you're in trouble. If you were speaking at a youth rally and you said, "Twenty-three skiddoo," you'd be laughed off the stage.

So the best advice about using slang is, "Of course, you can use it, but be careful, and use it only in its latest context and to the right group."

Laugh At Yourself Occasionally To Relieve Stuffiness. One of the tragedies of being pompous is that we—ourselves—don't realize it. Often we take ourselves too seriously, when we need to poke a little fun at ourselves. We need to laugh at ourselves, but we need to laugh with others also. Group laughter is group therapy—it's good medicine.

Audiences love to see a speaker laugh at himself when he makes a bobble or blooper. They like speakers who can make them laugh. Laughter nearly always gets rid of stuffiness. Solomon said, "A merry heart doeth good like medicine."

Do use illustrations

To illustrate means to light up or make clear. It's the most efficient way for a speaker to drive home a point. Illustrations are stories or examples. They're "for instances"; they're word pictures; they're attention-getters, and people remember them. But let me illustrate.

Two men went up into the temple to pray; the one a Pharisee, and the other a publican.

The Pharisee stood and prayed thus with himself, God, I thank thee, that I am not as other men are, extortioners, unjust, adulterers, or even as this publican.

I fast twice in the week, I give tithes of all that I possess.

And the publican, standing afar off would not lift up so much as his eyes unto heaven, but smote upon his breast, saying, God be merciful to me a sinner.

I tell you, this man went down to his house justified rather than the other: for every one that exalteth himself shall be abased; and he that humbleth himself shall be exalted.

The above parable is found in Luke 18:10-14.

Luke used verse 9 to tell why Jesus spoke this parable: "He spake this parable unto certain which trusted in themselves that they were righteous, and despised others." Jesus spoke this parable to teach and to make a clear point—and it did.

I used this quotation to show you the power of an illustration, example, or parable.

Good speakers use illustrations and examples to teach because nothing else is as effective. When you come right down to it, illustrations are about the only things that people do remember.

1. *Tell Me A Story!* If you have, or have had, small children, this request has been made of you many times. Children love to hear stories—ones with real names, plots that stretch their imagination, and end on a happy note. You'll never forget the story of the *Three Bears* or *Old Mother Hubbard*.

It always amazed me how fast children remember nursery rhymes and bedtime stories. And usually they'll never forget them, either. Why?

Rudolf Flesch says, "Only stories are remembered." This is true with your speaking. You'll be remembered to the degree that you are able to put your thoughts into stories, examples, and illustrations.

2. *Don't Preach—Teach.* One of the hardest things I have to do in my development class is to

get the men to use personal examples, instead of lecturing. They're instructed to teach by personal example instead of preaching, or in other words, to say, "Here's how I did it."

Positive teaching is done by example or illustration. It's to compare an unknown thing with a known thing. It's to hold up a picture and let the people identify with it.

One of the best examples of the power of illustrations is the manner in which the prophet Nathan approached David. This is found in II Samuel 12:1-7:

And the Lord sent Nathan unto David. And he came unto him, and said unto him, There were two men in one city; the one rich, and the other poor.

The rich man had exceeding many flocks and herds:

But the poor man had nothing, save one little ewe lamb, which he had brought and nourished up: and it grew up together with him, and with his children; it did eat of his own meat, and drank of his own cup, and lay in his bosom, and was unto him as a daughter.

And there came a traveller unto the rich man, and he spared to take of his own flock and of his own herd, to dress for the wayfaring man that was come unto him; but took the poor man's lamb, and dressed it for the man that was come to him.

And David's anger was greatly kindled against the man; and he said to Nathan, As the Lord liveth, the man that hath done this thing shall surely die:

And he shall restore the lamb fourfold, because he did this thing, and because he had no pity.

And Nathan said to David, Thou art the man.

See how much more impact this example had

upon David than if Nathan had only scolded him for his sin and told him that the Lord was going to kill the child? This left David with nothing to say except, "I have sinned against the Lord."

Illustrations and examples do help you speak so people will listen to you. So put your ideas into story form, give them a hero, and let him win against overwhelming odds. *People like stories where the good guys win.* We learn when speakers compare the unknown with the known by the use of examples, stories, and illustration. They'll make your talks *enjoyable* to your audience—and what's more, your listeners will *remember* what you say.

3. *People Like to Hear Dialogue And Quotations.* Have you ever thought why gossip is so popular? It's because it is about real people, using their own words, in their own setting. Real people say, "ain't"; they pause or hesitate, sip tea, and clear their throats. Much of this is revealed by using dialogue.

Which of the stories would catch your attention and make you listen?

The two women were talking on the telephone about ladies' Easter hats that were worn at the church services last Sunday.

Now, let's change this general, vague, and lifeless story to one of interest and color—one that you'd like to hear.

"Hello, Mable! Gotta minute?"

"Yeah, Marge. Hang on a second, let me get some more coffee."

"Sure."

"Okay, Marge, I'm on the other phone now."

"Where were you sitting in church yesterday?"

"Oh, near the back of the north side. Marvin had a headache."

"Well, what did you think of that sermon?"

"I guess it was O.K., but did you see that horrible hat that Millie Mae was wearing?"

"Yeah, the way it stuck out in back made her nose look even longer!"

"That poor Milton . . . all these years . . ."

"Uh-huh."

"And especially since little Mary ran away with that . . ."

See how dialogue and quotations catch and hold interest and attention? Use them often.

Don't be general and vague

Illustrations keep your speech from being general and vague. When you don't use examples, pictures, and here's-how-I-did-its, people will not understand you. Don't beat around the bush—come out with it. Get to the point—don't shadowbox, apologize, or pussy-foot around—get to the point!

Let your audience *feel* the bone-crushing auto accident that you're describing. Help them *visualize* that mountain stream. Put some jagged rocks in it and some golden aspen leaves along its bank. *Describe* that scroungy, hungry, dirty, gray mutt that whimpered at your door during a thunderstorm. *Feel, smell, taste,* and *visualize* —these are what an audience likes to do when you speak.

Don't be general and vague.

Do outline your talk

Many speakers boast about not using outlines while they speak. Some speak effectively without an outline, but others ramble, shuffle, and repeat themselves. Unless you're an accomplished speaker, you should prepare and follow an outline. *An outline can crystalize your thinking as nothing else will.* Your goal is still to get your message into the minds of your listeners, not to belong to an elite non-outline-user club.

You can make a thorough outline while preparing your talk, and then make a simple version of it to use in delivering your speech. Or you may use the complete outline while speaking. Whatever your personal needs and likes are, you'll profit by using some sort of an outline. The use of a well prepared outline will help your speech be conversational. You'll have more confidence in delivery, knowing that if you strike out mentally, you can quickly find home base again.

Here is an example of a complete outline that I recently prepared.

HOW TO MOTIVATE
THE BIBLE SCHOOL MEMBER

ATTENTION

The job of the successful teacher is to make the student *want* to learn!
1. Unless you do this, there is no learning.
2. So then, teaching becomes basically motivation.
3. They'll forget 95% of what you tell them.
4. You must teach them to dig it out for themselves.
5. Motivation is the biggest problem in the business world today!

IMPORTANCE

You must learn to *motivate* the members to be a successful teacher!

EXAMPLES

I. First you must have confidence in yourself—this is catching and obvious to the students.
   A. This means prayer—before, during, and after preparation.
      1. Take advantage of this strength.
      2. You're not the success that you could be if you don't.
   B. Know your lesson—this means preparation.
      1. Store up data and extra knowledge.
      2. Know that you know it.
      3. Know you know it better than anyone else at that time.
   C. Welcome "pre-game" nervousness.
II. Do these things and you'll successfully handle people:
      Don't criticize, but point out good traits.
      Don't give up on people, but encourage them.

Don't take remarks personally, but expect ingratitude.

A. Don't criticize, but point out good traits.
   1. A study was made among school children who were working math problems.
      a. Mistakes noted—20% gain.
      b. Commended for sums correct—70% gain.
   2. Do you really like "constructive criticism"? Now be honest, do you?
      a. No, most of us don't.
      b. We are well aware of our faults.
   3. When our good points are pointed out we always respond with cooperation and we try harder.
   4. Lincoln said: "A drop of honey catches more flies than a gallon of gall."
B. Don't give up on people, but encourage them.
   1. Man is not primarily a creature of logic, but of emotion.
      a. God made man to:
         (1) Hunger for a feeling of worth.
         (2) Feel a need for appreciation.
      b. Man needs recognition and acceptance.
   2. Those "too dumb to learn" boys may grow up to be Thomas Edisons.
      a. Edison was kicked out of school because his teacher thought he was too dumb to learn.
      b. He found the inner drive to succeed because of encouragement and education from his mother.
      c. How many other potential Edisons have been permanently thwarted by criticism?
   3. Except for low mentality, all of your class members can achieve great things.
   4. Look back on your own life: your successes and victories have come because someone had faith in you and encouraged you.

       5. William James said, "The deepest principle in human nature is the craving to be appreciated."

       6. If you're not taking advantage of this tool, you're not teaching effectively.

C. Don't take remarks personally, but expect ingratitude.

       1. Jesus healed 10 lepers one afternoon.

          a. Now think of the magnitude of this miracle.

          b. How much would each have paid to be cured?

          c. But what happened *after* they were healed?

       2. I read that Andrew Carnegie left a relative one million dollars.

          a. How would you feel if a rich uncle had done this to you?

          b. How do you suppose this person felt?

          c. Thankful? No, he later cursed Carnegie because he had left $365 million to other charities and cut him off with a measly million dollars.

       3. Now my point is that if we expect gratitude, we will suffer many heartaches.

       4. When we expect ingratitude, we continue along our course undisturbed—content with our own knowledge of accomplishment.

       5. So, expect ingratitude—realize that critical remarks are often compliments in disguise—and you'll not have ulcers.

CONCLUSION

    1. Make these points your rule.

       a. Have faith in people.

       b. Have confidence in their future.

       c. Let them know you do.

     d. Believe that good seeds planted will eventually produce good fruits.

     e. Think in terms of the individual.

  2. Shoot for the 70% improvement.

     a. Don't criticize, but point out good traits.

     b. Don't give up on people, but encourage them.

     c. Don't take remarks personally, but expect ingratitude.

  3. Do these things and you'll *successfully* handle people and *motivate* your members.

This is a very complete outline. You may not want to detail yours to this extent, or you may want to make a smaller outline from this one. You can do this by simply crossing out some of the subtopics.

Now notice the mechanics of this outline. The major divisions are the ones listed in Chapter 3. They are: *Attention, Importance, Examples*, and *Conclusion*. The points under Attention, Importance, and Conclusion are indicated simply by 1, 2, and 3. The body, or examples, is broken down into Roman numerals I, II and III. Here is an example of the organization under each Roman numeral.

I.

   A.

      1.

         a.

           (1)

             (a)

I prefer to make a detailed outline during

preparation and use the same one while delivering a talk. It isn't necessary to look at all the subtopics, because I know what they are; but if I get hung up, it's easy to find the right track again.

Remember, a good outline will crystalize your thinking during preparation. It will help you eliminate shuffling and repetition. With its use, you can be a confident conversational speaker.

Don't write out your talk word for word

It's usually murder for a speaker to attempt to deliver a speech that he has written out word for word. The fact is that we don't usually write like we talk. Unless we have worked hours on this, our writing is much more pompous and ivory-towered than our talking. There are two dangers in writing out a talk word for word. They are:

(1) lack of conversational tone to voice when delivering, and

(2) the ease of losing your place when speaking.

It's rare to find a person who can read in the same manner that he talks. Emphasis and inflection are never right. You can easily detect the person who is reading a prepared speech. He doesn't have the listening appeal of the conversational speaker.

There's nothing more blurred than a written manuscript when a speaker has lost his place. If this has ever happened to you, you know exactly the feeling and the utter horror. Then the more you try to find it, the more difficult it is to locate.

The quick and best advice is simply not to write out your talk word for word. Do this and you'll stay out of hot water—outline your talks and you'll gain ease and confidence.

Chapter Eight

Potpourri

Potpourri means a mixture, or medley, or anthology. So then, this chapter is a mixture of suggestions and ideas. These ideas will help you gain confidence and do a better job of speaking. And even more important, when you use them you'll get along better with people.

How to shake hands

Let's do some thinking about the down-to-earth subject of handshaking. It's very important to you because it reveals much of your confidence and personality. Your confidence in speaking and handshaking go together, and one complements the other. You'll also find this a good way to build up your confidence.

Now there are several bad handshakes, but probably the two worst ones are the "half-gottchi" and the "old cold fish."

How do you feel when you reach for someone's hand and all of sudden, before your palms meet, they've locked down on your four fingers? There you stand; they've got you, but you don't have them. This always startles me, and indicates to me an obvious lack of manliness, sincerity, and interest. Notice also that this type usually doesn't look in your eye. You feel that he's not really interested in you. He's usually distant, standoffish, and doesn't express himself or reveal his feelings. He lacks confidence.

Similarly, and probably more common, is the "old cold fish." It hasn't been too long since you've had someone slither a mackerel-cold hand into yours, has it? Remember how there was no feeling of sincerity or warmth? The fellow didn't seem too interested in you, did he? Chances are he didn't make a good impression either. The tragedy of this type of handshake is that it reflects a complete lack of confidence.

On the other hand, a good, firm, sincere handshake shows confidence, but even more it's a con-

fidence builder. It keeps your level of self-value up and tells everyone, "I consider myself valuable and important, but I'm just as interested in you." Feel on the same level with the other person; don't talk up or down to him. Never bend toward a man when you shake his hand, because the moment you do, you get off his level.

When you shake someone's hand, stand tall. Look him in the eye. Let your hand go all the way into his, until the valley between your index finger and thumb meets the same part of his hand. Clasp his hand in a firm and sincere way. Hold it two or three seconds and then let go. That's enough! It can be overdone, and it's embarrassing for someone to hold on to your hand too long. You never seem to know what to do.

Along with this, it's important to get eye contact with the person when shaking his hand. Most of us don't do this properly. Many people look at the other person's lips when they shake hands. Some will try to look at both eyes, and then settle by keeping their eyes on the bridge of his nose. The best way is to pick out just one eye, usually the right one, and look into it.

This will make an impact on the person as nothing else will. It's piercing, it commands the person's attention, and it shows confidence. It's difficult to do and will take some concentration on your part, but it's worth the effort. When you shake hands with someone, *make an impact on them*, and you can do this by establishing eye contact with them. Try it!

Frequently men ask me what to do about shaking a woman's hand. I'm not sure that we can deal in absolutes, but here are a couple of suggestions that will help. Number one, shake hands with a lady only if she wants to. Let her call the shots or start the action. A lot of women don't like to shake a man's hand. You can tell quickly if she wants to shake your hand or not. If she makes no move, then you can just nod or bend slightly and look into her eyes.

If a lady wants to shake your hand and initiates the action, here's a suggestion of how to hold her hand. Don't hold her hand like you would a man's. Hold her four fingers in the palm of your hand with your thumb just above her large knuckles, then slightly squeeze her fingertips with your third and little fingers. This type of handshake can be done without hurting the lady or putting too much pressure on her hand. But remember—the most important item is to establish eye contact. Get her attention for just a few seconds, and you'll force her to concentrate on you and remember you.

The handshake is a very important act in our lives. With it we convey our feelings to one another, but it also gives a hint of the person we are. We show our confidence, or lack of it, by our handshake. This is an art, and we build our confidence when we do it properly. If you deal with people (and who doesn't?), it's important that you know how to shake hands with them.

Try this interesting experiment. For the next three weeks shake as many hands as possible and keep a record of the effective encounters. Then make a mental note of the poor ones. It will be a rather revealing experiment—you'll make some new friends, you'll inject new confidence in others, and at the same time build up your own. And what's more, you'll have a good time doing it.

Look your best and boost your confidence

You are judged by your appearance! Right or wrong, and whether you like it or not, this is true. While this isn't always a correct way to measure a man, it does tip off the habits and confidence of the person. Your appearance broadcasts to others the type of person you are.

A low self-image is often revealed by dressing in a sloppy manner or by over-dressing. The "Sloppy Joe" doesn't think much of himself. Neither does the "Natty Norman," but he tries to over-compensate for his feeling of inferiority by calling attention to his dress.

How you look outside affects the way you feel inside! Proper dressing can help you a great deal by giving your confidence a boost. Remember how great you felt the last time you wore that new suit? But remember, good dressing doesn't call attention to itself. It's the sum of several parts, all integrated into a well displayed whole.

Good dressing involves paying attention to little things. Ever see someone wear a new, nice looking suit with a wilted and dingy shirt? It ruined the whole effect, didn't it? Notice the little things. Keep your pant cuffs clean and notice the crease in them before you wear them. Wear socks that are long enough so when you cross your legs you don't show a shiny shin. A crisply starched shirt looks better than a wilted one. Choose your ties carefully because they tip off your taste.

When I was in college, one of my roommates was an exceptionally good dresser. He always looked neat. He was well-groomed; his suits, ties, shirts, shoes, and socks always matched, without any of them calling attention to themselves. He didn't have too many clothes, but those he had were good, and he took care to properly hang them after each wearing.

Since that time, I've learned that it's better to have fewer clothes—but have better ones. You're actually money ahead to have two $125 suits than four $65 ones. You'll enjoy them more and they'll last longer.

The best advice I've ever had about dressing was to pick out a good clothing salesman and do all my business with him. I let him know how much I can afford and then listened to his advice.

Furthermore, he always let me know when a sale was coming so I could take advantage of it.

But watch out for sales; the most expensive suits that I've ever bought were the ones that I didn't particularly like, but I just couldn't pass up the bargain. Grit your teeth and pay a little more than usual for a new suit; it'll hurt some when you do, but you'll be glad later.

In short, cut down on the quantity and pay more attention to the quality—and you'll be money ahead. Buy half as many and pay twice the price is good advice.

A car dealer once told me that, "Almost everybody secretly desires to take an occasional drive in a yellow convertible." He meant that most people secretly desire to step out of character briefly and splurge. To what extent this is true, I don't know, but I suppose most men are tempted to buy a rather bold and flamboyant sport coat sometimes. I'm sure you've had occasional thoughts like this yourself, and if you yielded you might have been a little uncomfortable in it. Don't be a "Colorless Clarence," but don't over-dress either. Be comfortable in your clothes and you'll be more confident in your attitudes and actions.

Another thing that'll help you look your best is to *get a hair cut before you need one*. This will probably mean once a week. The important thing is to set a schedule and follow it. When you can tell that you need a haircut, it's too late. I learned this from a deliveryman who worked for me several years ago. His hair always looked the same—well-groomed and clean. It never seemed to grow out and look shaggy. I complimented him one day on this, and he told me that he went to the barber shop once a week. Doing this will add a little to the budget, but it'll be worth it.

Alexander Pope once wrote: "Be not the first by whom the new are tried, nor yet the last to lay the old aside." This is good advice in your dress, as in many other areas of your life. Stay in style, but make sure your clothes are well in style before you buy them.

When you dress confidently and comfortably, you'll command the respect of others more, and they'll listen to what you have to say.

How to carry on a conversation without being a bore

The main reason some people aren't good conversationalists is because they try too hard. Many of us think we must tell of some big deal that we've pulled in order to impress others. But let's face it, when we do this, we're just plain bores.

The best way to carry on a conversation without being a bore is to *talk about the other person*, or about his interests. This requires a lot of listening. People want to tell you of their accomplishments and interests, not listen to yours. Good conversationalists take advantage of this fact.

Several years ago, I owned a small contemporary furniture business. I was in Dallas on a buying trip and had a luncheon appointment with a Swedish industrialist named Folke Ohlsson. Mr. Ohlsson was the president of a world-wide furniture building concern, whose salary was probably twice the salary of the President of the United States. He had worked his way up from a cleanup boy to a company president. He was a genius at furniture design, with many of them winning world acclaim. In fact, as I recall, one of them had won an award at the Brussel's World's Fair just before our meeting. He was the first person to successfully market Scandinavian furniture in the United States on a broad scale.

Looking back on that visit, I can see the real lesson behind his ability at conversation, and I can see why Mr. Ohlsson had achieved success. He was at ease around people, and he knew how to carry on a conversation.

As we were seated at our table, Mr. Ohlsson's first words were, "Mr. Willingham, how do you think we can improve our products?"

Wow! Do you know I was so impressed with his awareness of rare intelligence that I spent almost two hours telling him how he could improve his products.

He listened very intently, and when I'd exhaust my knowledge on a particular subject (which was fairly often), he'd simply ask another question. He followed my endless patter with patience and an occasional nod of agreement. I was sure, from the way he listened, that he had tapped the greatest source of furniture knowledge to be found. What a bore I must have been! But for months, all I thought about was what a tremendous conversationalist Folke Ohlsson was and how interested he was in me.

Mr. Ohlsson had learned a secret that it was to take me several years to learn—that a good conversationalist is someone who is a good listener. Also, he is someone who is interested in other people and can ask well placed questions.

Last week I was drinking coffee with six or seven men, and someone mentioned having the flu during the past week. He told how sick he was, how long he was in bed, and all about his temperature. Before he could finish, one of the other men broke into the conversation with an account of his bout with the flu. Glancing around the table at the men, I saw that each man was just itching to tell about his last illness. I also noticed that not a single man was permitted to finish his story before he was interrupted by another who was sicker and had higher temperature. It was clear that no one was really interested in the other man's illness; each was only interested in telling of his own.

Nobody likes to hear about your illness. You'll not interest anyone by telling about your operation, or by showing them your scar. We're so captivated with ourselves that we think other people should be interested also, but they aren't.

It's tough advice to take, but don't talk about your ailments. And especially to your poor wife . . . she's heard enough now to last a lifetime!

If you want to be an expert conversationalist, and one that other people really enjoy being around, then follow this simple formula: *Ask questions and listen.* This is a sure-fire way to gain the respect of others. The less you have to say, the better conversationalist you appear to others. And the more questions you ask, the more interest you show.

I like to run an occasional experiment when I'm with another person for any length of time. I simply ask questions and listen. It's amazing how well I get to know some people this way, and it's even more amazing how it helps them. The payoff comes when they suddenly apologize for doing all the talking. Usually it's phrased like this, "I'm sorry *if* I've done all the talking." When I hear this remark, I know I've been a successful conversationalist.

While strengthening your listening habits, here are three things not to do while you're talking: (1) Don't gossip. This never does anything but get you into trouble. We do it to strengthen our own position, but it never does.

(2) Don't give advice unless someone asks for it. And usually the person who seeks it only wants you to agree with him. If you want to stay out of trouble, don't give advice freely. (3) Never be sarcastic. Benjamin Franklin once observed that this is folly, and that the person who uses it neither improves others, is improved himself, nor pleases anyone. In other words, it benefits no one and is a good way to lose a friend or audience.

Let me sum this all up by saying: *Don't try to be a good conversationalist; be a good listener.* Don't talk about your terrible bout with the flu last week, or show that jagged scar, or narrate that near-death operation. Don't gossip, give advice, or be sarcastic. Observe these things and you'll be welcomed anywhere, and you'll be amazed at your newly acquired popularity.

How to compliment someone— sincerely

Have you ever noticed how neglected this art is, and yet how everyone hungers for appreciation? You'd think that since it's free, it would be more common. But the law of supply and demand doesn't work here. The supply is unlimited, as is the demand, but the actual rate of exchange is amazingly low.

There are so few people who really practice this trait, that when we do develop it, we immediately place ourselves in a rare and elite group.

Proper application of this will feed our confidence, and what's more, we'll be welcome guests in any crowd.

Most of us would like to be a compliment-giver, but many times we're afraid that it will be misunderstood and taken as cheap flattery. One reason for our hesitation is that we don't know exactly how the recipient will accept our praise.

At times our appreciation may not be accepted because it is too general. The secret is to be specific and point out why we appreciate something or someone. Instead of just saying, "Boy, you sure look nice today," you could be more *specific* and say, "Sam, your tie goes exceptionally well with that suit. The colors blend beautifully."

Or instead of mumbling to your wife, "Sure enjoyed the meal," you could tell her *why* you enjoyed it by saying, "The spaghetti sauce was very good, and I especially enjoyed the mushrooms in it."

When we appreciate something, there has to be a *reason*. So, look for the reason and *mention* it. This gives our praise and appreciation meaning and keeps it from being taken as cheap flattery.

I once read that *we increase whatever we praise*. And it's true. But instead of believing this, some of us go through life feeling that it is harmful to puff up other people and contaminate them with a feeling of their own importance.

"After all," we say, "it's wrong to be filled with pride." Unfortunately, when we tell ourselves this, we not only deceive ourselves and go against our own self-feeling, but we rob ourselves of one of the most powerful and potent ways to motivate and influence others. Praise is powerful. It moves men. With a sincere application of it we become leaders—not drivers or followers.

During the third week of my development course, the men are given an action guide to practice for a couple of weeks. The guide goes like this:

EVERY DAY,
AT LEAST ONCE,
SINCERELY
COMPLIMENT SOMEONE

At first many of the men think it sounds a little Pollyanna, or idealistic, and occasionally, we note some skeptical reactions. But, whenever a person practices this technique, he becomes hooked and sees how powerful it is.

One evening, Frank Landon, who is the manager of a Safeway supermarket, told me that practicing this caused him to give raises to four employees. This seemed like a rather unusual result, but he explained, "I have fifteen employees, some are new and inexperienced. They make a lot of mistakes and foul up a lot of things. I'd always seen the mistakes that they made and pointed them out. On the other hand, I hadn't recognized their good traits, and the good that they were doing for the store. Then I changed my attitude and started looking for good in them and began to point this out instead of griping about their faults. I discovered that their attitudes improved, and that the store began to run a lot smoother. The employees became more friendly with each other and with the customers. This will help each person, as well as the company. And, I'm going to continue to practice this very important principle."

This principle will change your life, if you'll only apply it. Try it for three weeks and it'll become a part of you. Soon it will be so ingrained in your mind that it becomes automatic.

Last week I stopped in a service station in another town to get gasoline. The restroom was exceptionally clean, with soap and towels, a large mirror, and it was well-lighted. It was obvious that the owner was a hard worker and took pride in his business. When I paid for the gasoline, I said, "I really appreciate the cleanliness of your restroom. It's refreshing to wash my hands and face and know that every thing is clean."

You'd have thought the attendant had inherited a million dollars. He put on a broad smile, stiffened his shoulders, and said, "Well, we do try. But you know, a lot of people don't appreciate our efforts."

When I drove off the man was standing on the driveway, smiling and waving. I'll probably never see him again and will never know how much the compliment boosted him that day; but when I've forgotten about praising his efforts, he'll still remember it.

There's something lasting about a compliment. The giver may immediately forget that he gave it, but the receiver will not. I can remember compliments given to me twenty-five years ago. In some cases, I can remember the exact words, but cannot recall the name of the giver. It's amazing how our subconscious mind retains these pleasant memories and lets us feed off of them when we need strength and encouragement.

Of course, my point is that we should remember the power of such gestures of kindness and understand how much genuine, sincere appreciation helps others. It's one of our most potent and effective tools in motivating and building others—and always remember: *We ourselves succeed in direct proportion to the help we give others.*

Another effective way to show appreciation is to *write a short note to someone who has done a good job on something.* Many times this is more effective a than verbal compliment because the recipient doesn't have to show his embarrassment in receiving it. Also, he can read it several times and really relish it. Use a very simple outline, such as this:

1. Thank the person for his deed of kindness.
2. Tell how it has helped you.
3. Thank him again.

I keep some fold-over notes and envelopes in my desk and briefcase. It's so easy to jot down a long-hand note, address it, and drop it into the mail. However, you must do it immediately while your appreciation is fresh in your mind.

These are just a few suggestions that will help you grow in the ability to give praise and appreciation to others. I'm sure that you know of several others. But simply knowing isn't enough; *action* is the thing! You'll enjoy this delightful experiment in abundant living.

Praise does magnify the good quality of others; it builds up other people. But more important—it builds you up at the same time.

How to accept a compliment

While cultivating the healthy habit of giving sincere praise and appreciation, it's also important that we learn how to receive and accept compliments. *For to graciously receive a compliment is to give one back to the giver.* But few people really know how to do this important thing. Instead, we tend to slough off praise and yell long and loud that we're not worthy of it. This not only spoils the pleasure of the giver and closes the door for future signs of appreciation, but it shows our own lack of confidence.

Our self-confidence can also be measured by the way we accept compliments, and it's true, too, that we can bolster our confidence by building up our ability to accept praise and appreciation. Don't you feel empty when you give someone a compliment and they have the attitude, "Naw, you don't mean me . . . you're just joking . . . don't try to con me, buddy . . . Me! oh, surely not me . . . etc."? Without thinking, many people seem to question your sincerity.

In our development classes the members vote each evening for the outstanding speaker, and he is awarded a nice book or a pocket size New Testament. Recently, a man was given an award, and this in substance is what he said, "Well, I'm sure everybody is going to get one of these sooner or later, and I guess I might as well get mine tonight. Besides, you probably felt sorry for me anyway."

What had been happiness for a deserving fellow turned into disappointment, and this punctured the enthusiasm of the whole class—all because of his lack of confidence. Incidentally, I am happy to say that in the next few weeks this man did strengthen his self-image and gained a tremendous amount of self-confidence. This happened when he stopped thinking about his own little narrow world and got interested in other people and their interests. And I noticed that as his own confidence was strengthened, he began encouraging other men in the group more and more. In reality, both of these grew in direct proportion to each other, and each fed the other.

Personally, I like to mentally associate accepting a compliment with a football team. Picture the team in a set position, the center is over the ball, and snaps it to the quarterback. The quarterback takes the ball, holds it momentarily, and then usually hands it off or passes it.

Now assume the ball is the compliment, the center is the giver, and the quarterback is the receiver. Let's tie it together by remembering when someone gives us a compliment, we accept it and keep it momentarily. We acknowledge that we have it and thank the giver, but then we can either hand it off, or pass it, by giving credit to others.

The secret is to accept the compliment, but not to keep it to ourselves. Don't pass it back to the giver or fumble it, but with confidence and grace, give someone else a pat on the back. For example, "Thank you, we are proud of our beautiful flower garden. My wife planted all the bulbs herself." Or, "I enjoy this suit, too, thanks to a good salesman who has been helping me select my clothes for several years."

Chapter Nine

Who's going to use your talents but you?

Lincoln once said: *"I'll study and get ready, and then maybe my chance will come."* These are wise and true words. But to go even further, it's necessary that we prepare and be ready or we'll not even *recognize* a chance or opportunity. Opportunity is only opportunity when we have adequately prepared for it.

The reason that many of us don't succeed in life is because we haven't prepared ourselves for success. James Allen, in his classic book, *As A Man Thinketh*, said: "Men are anxious to improve their circumstances, but are unwilling to improve themselves; they therefore remain bound."

Today, many of us are living proof of Mr. Allen's statement. We want advancement and accomplishment without preparation. We want the good things of life, but don't want to work for them. But try as we may, we can't change the law.

Preparation involves many things. It begins with a desire for improvement and the setting of definite, specific goals. It means work. It takes study and concentration. Self-discipline is a must. It's necessary that we weed out our ineffective actions and habits. We must couple preparation with a strong belief that we *can* improve and achieve greater goals.

These things are essential, but you'll need something else. Many people study and prepare themselves but, unfortunately, they stop there and go no farther. There's another side to the coin—*action*.

In our development classes I usually point out that nothing new will be learned, but we will learn how to apply what we already know. One evening I received this response from a fellow named Al Wilson. Al said, "I ain't puttin' into practice everything I know now, so I reckon knowledge ain't so important as just a gettin' to work."

This comment showed an insight that is lacking in many people of great learning. It is practical and true and hits at the heart of much of our problem.

Action is the thing

James, the New Testament writer, says that "Faith without works is dead." And so is *knowledge* without *action*—it's lifeless and stale.

Things are done by doers. Empires are built by men of action. Desire is important but is passive—*action is the thing*.

Likely, the doers that you know aren't the most brilliant men among your friends. Edison was kicked out of school because his teachers thought he was too dumb to learn. But he was a man of action—a doer. If any man ever had reason to lie down and quit, it was Lincoln. It's likely that no other famous person suffered comparable failures. He was a *dreamer*, but he was also a *doer*—and that's the important thing. The Apostle Paul "was not an eloquent speaker" and yet he was a great one—he was a doer.

I have a friend, Scotty Witt, who came out of the army ten years ago with the idea of establishing a youth camp. I laughed at him at first. He spent several months looking for possible sites and finally found one in northeastern New Mexico. It was a beautiful twelve hunddred acre ranch in the Sangre De Cristo Mountains and was priced at seventy-five thousand dollars.

But he didn't even have a thousand dollars.

Scotty promptly told the owners that he would buy the ranch, and they agreed to a twenty thousand dollar down payment, which, of course, he didn't have.

He obtained some time to raise the down payment, and took time from his business to solicit contributions from interested individuals.

I thought he had lost his mind and was sure that he couldn't raise that kind of money. Most other people felt the same way because he only received small contributions. This made it more difficult to accumulate the down payment, but it didn't dampen his spirits. I've never seen anyone work so hard, and in a few months he had the down payment and the camp was purchased.

He got busy and sold beautiful cabin sites along a stream. This helped pay off the mortgage. Now, ten years later, the camp is paid for, has been improved, and is worth around two hundred and fifty thousand dollars. About eight hundred young people enjoy the mountains and nature each summer, and over thirty families enjoy their cabins. And this number includes our family.

All of this happened, not because of excess intelligence (I can testify to that), but because Scotty Witt was a *doer*. The people who get on in this world are the ones who dream and see possibilities—then go out and do something about it. Things are done by doers.

Shakespeare once said, "Our doubts are traitors and make us lose the good we oft might win by fearing to attempt." When many of us get a good idea, or at least what seems like a good idea at the time, and don't act immediately, doubt starts to set in. We start thinking of all the reasons why something won't work instead of the reasons why it will work. Then we talk ourselves out of even trying.

Let me share an example of this with you. For a number of months I have been wanting a new Mercedes-Benz 250S automobile. The only problem is that I can't afford one.

About a month ago I suddenly had an idea. Since I had no money to buy the car, why not trade my services for it? I could hold a sales and human relations meeting once a week for the dealer in return for the use of the car.

My first reaction was to rush out and discuss this with the dealer. I had all kinds of confidence. Then the thought occurred that maybe there were some holes in my thinking and that I should wait three or four days, think about it, and see if I still thought it was a good idea.

You know what? In three days, the idea didn't seem nearly as logical as it did at first, and I thought I'd better wait a little longer. So, I waited, and each day I became more convinced that the idea was a little far-fetched. However, a couple of times I started to go out and talk to the dealer, but balked each time because of lack of confidence and decisiveness. I could think of a dozen reasons why he wouldn't be interested. Then I wasn't sure that it would be worth my time to do it. Doubts, doubts, doubts!

Finally, last week I thought, "Ole boy, this idea has been bugging you for a month now. You'll never be satisfied until you find out, so get with it and go ask."

So I did, and the owner agreed that he needed this type of training for his salesmen. He had some reorganization to do, and in about a month he'd like to start this training. Now, I can only assume this will work out, but it certainly never would have if I hadn't taken action and asked. And even if it falls through, the important thing is that I gained a victory the moment I applied *action*.

Now you're probably wondering whether or not I can deliver the goods and increase his sales. Right? Well, of course, only time will tell, but you know what the first lesson will be? That's right—*action!*

Incidentally, how many auto salesmen have ever called you and visited with you *after* the sale was made? How many want to know if your car is running right, or if there is anything they can do to help you and serve you? How many really follow up *after* the sale is made?

If you're like the fifty people that I've interviewed, the odds are 8 to 2 that this has never happened to you. And most of these people said that they would have bought their next car from the last salesman who sold them, *if* he had followed up and shown some *interest* in them.

80% of the people didn't buy their last automobile from the same salesman who sold them one previously. In other words, there was no loyalty to the salesman. Why? Because they didn't feel the salesman was interested in them. Why? Lack of action! Lack of action on the salesman's part, that is. There's really no competition for the salesman who's honest, friendly, and interested in *serving* you. Is there?

How many times have you said, "I can't"? How many times do you fail to attempt? We fail to attempt because we're afraid of failure, thereby losing the "good we oft might win." The "fearing to attempt" that Shakespeare wrote about is the very opposite of action. Action is the final expression of the desire to attempt. It is courage put to work. *Action does take courage, but the rewards are many.*

Emerson once said, "Do the thing and you'll have the power." How true this is! How many times have you launched out and attempted; then suddenly found that you *can* do the thing? Of course, what Emerson is saying is that we can do a lot of things when we actually try.

Action, action, action! Action is the thing. Cultivate the "do-it-now habit," and you'll cultivate the success habit. It's very important—your future success depends upon it!

Desire, knowledge, and finally *action*. It takes all three, but the greatest of these is *action*.

So you've got a handicap—let it help you!

The Apostle Paul had a "thorn in the flesh." It could have been a speech impediment or crossed eyes. The Scriptures indicate that this helped him gain a true perspective of himself. It helped him become a more mature Christian. In II Corinthians 12:9, Paul asked God to remove the thorn, but God answered:

> My grace is sufficient for thee: for my strength is made perfect in weakness. Most gladly therefore will I rather glory in my infirmities, that the power of Christ may rest upon me. Therefore I take pleasure in infirmities, in reproaches, in necessities, in persecutions, in distresses for Christ's sake: for when I am weak, then am I strong.

Paul had learned the valuable lesson that handicaps strengthen us.

Demosthenes overcame great difficulties to become a great Greek orator. At first he had a harsh unpleasant voice, weak lungs, and an awkward manner. But he recited as he climbed steep mountains. He shouted above the roar of ocean waves with pebbles in his mouth. His handicap helped him to become great.

It's said that *Winston Churchill overcame great difficulties in learning to speak well*. He was plagued with a lisp and a stutter in his younger years. He overcame them and became one of the greatest speakers of this century.

Dr. Rollo May wrote in his excellent book, *The Art of Counseling*, the following paragraph about suffering:

Suffering is one of the most potentially creative forces in nature. It is not sentimentality to relate the greatness of certain characters to their sufferings. As the pearl is produced in the endeavor of the clam to adjust itself to the irritation of the grain of sand, so the great works of Poe and Shelley and Van Gogh and Dostoevski are understandable only in relation to the suffering these artists experienced.

People should then rejoice in suffering, strange as it sounds, for this is the sign of the availability of energy to transform their characters.

So you've got a handicap! Let it help you achieve your best. It will, if you'll only cooperate. And you can learn to become a successful speaker, or a successful anything, if you'll only try.

So clearly do I see this proven in our development classes. I see men come into it with problems and handicaps that have hampered them all their lives. When they accept their "thorns in the flesh," they gain confidence with self-value. Dozens of lisps, stutterings, and voice hesitations disappear when people forget themselves and realize that they can overcome these things.

I recall one man with a hare-lip who constantly rubbed the bottom of his nose with his index finger. This was an automatic movement to cover his lip with his hand. The moment he realized that no one considered this a roadblock to friendship, he unconsciously quit rubbing his nose and dropped his hands to his side. This man held several jobs, and is now an executive director of a local community service organization. He has ability and is using it.

Another man in one of the classes had a malformed right hand. The hand has two fingers and a thumb, all twisted together. He came into the class with an extreme amount of self-consciousness and a very low self-image. When he made his talks, he would hold the deformed hand behind him. Later he started holding it just above his belt buckle with his left hand covering or hiding it. He wouldn't look directly at the audience, had little facial expression, and was scared to death.

When he began to gain a true self-concept, he started showing his withered hand. This true self-concept is built on a proper understanding that he is accepted by the other men for what he is. When he really understood this fact, his life began to change.

Soon he wasn't covering his hand at all, and then one night he got so excited that he started pounding it into the palm of his left hand to make a point. And, of course, when he did this, his face lighted up and he began accepting himself for what he is He now has friends because he shows himself friendly. He has discovered abilities that he never thought he had.

Recently, I asked this man what he was gaining from the class. This is part of his reply: "I have gained enthusiasm and confidence in myself. I enjoy being around people now. I don't mind shaking hands with people. I can look a person in the eye and still think of what I'm going to say." This man has done a great job in the class because he has let his handicap give him the drive to achieve.

One reason we often feel inferior is because we think certain handicaps limit us. I suppose that *almost every living person thinks he has some kind of physical handicap*. It's true that some are real, but many are imaginary.

Often we think we're too short, our nose is too large, or we're overweight. If I asked you if you have a physical feature that you'd like to change, you'd probably nod your head up and down. And yet, our "thorns in the flesh" usually prove to be assets. They usually help us achieve something good. So whatever you feel is your handicap—don't wish it away, but be thankful for it. Think for a few moments and you'll see how it has helped you. Do this and you'll count your blessings, not your troubles.

Now let's talk about you

God created you and gave you the power to become. *You can be anything you want to be.*

There's no limit, no ceiling, to the accomplishments that you can make—if you want to and are willing to work.

The Bible speaks of the one talent man. Today, many people think they have but one talent, only to find out differently after they've attempted to improve themselves. There's probably not a one talent person in every thousand people—I mean a person who only has one talent, and who will never have more.

We sell ourselves short. We habitually fail to accomplish goals that we're capable of attaining.

Regardless of who you are, what your present station is in life, or your background, you can gain a new life by daily attention and action.

Ralph Waldo Emerson was correct when he penned these words:

Do not wish for self-confidence . . . get it from within. Nobody can give it to you. It is one of the greatest assets of life. Self-confidence comes to you every time you are knocked down and get up. A little boy was asked how he learned to skate: "Oh, by getting up every time I fell down," he replied.

Opportunity is where you are. Weak men wait for opportunities; strong men make them. Self-trust is the first secret of success.

So look for these opportunities. When there's a job for you to do, do it. You may just be the only human who can do it. Your talents and abilities are unique and individual—God made us all that way. Also, remember that education never ends for the alert individual. We learn each day.

You can learn to express yourself better in all areas of your life. That's why you've read this book. That's why I have written it—to help you lead a more dynamic and purposeful life through better self-expression. If you really want to:

You can teach that Sunday school class.
You can preside at that luncheon.
You can make a more effective sales presentation.
You can make an effective talk.
You can improve your lot in life.

You can do these things if you really want to!

Speaking will bring you many rewards and benefits—ones that you've always wanted. You'll get a thrill out of speaking that comes no other way. Most truly successful people get that way by improving their ability to express themselves. Effective self-expression precedes success in most any field. So as you grow in this ability:

You'll immediately become a leader.
You'll increase your income.
You'll be more effective at human relations.
You'll be happier.
You'll gain self-confidence and courage.
You'll become a winner.

So *prepare* yourself to recognize opportunities, and then get busy. Remember, *action* is the thing. Forget your handicaps, dwell constantly on the rewards because:

God hath not given us the spirit of fear: but of power, and of love, and of a sound mind.